SKY FEVER

SKY FEVER

THE *AUTOBIOGRAPHY* OF

SIR GEOFFREY DE HAVILLAND

C.B.E.

Airlife

England

Airlife Publications

7 St. John's Hill, Shrewsbury, England.

Printed by Livesey Limited, Shrewsbury, England.

FOR JOAN
WITH LOVE

PREFACE

THIS book is not the story of the de Havilland Aircraft Company, for a very complete history has already been written by Martin Sharp. This is an autobiography in which I write of some of the more important and best remembered happenings in my long life, describing only in passing a few of the more outstanding of our aircraft. In Martin Sharp's history all the many aircraft we have designed are given, with full particulars.

What I most regret is the impossibility of paying tribute to the host of people without whose help my work in aviation could never have been accomplished. This applies to the earliest days at Stag Lane right up to the present time, and includes all members of the de Havilland enterprise, whatever status they may hold, and members of all our overseas companies, many of whom are my close friends. I can only extend to one and all my sincere thanks for the great contribution they have made by their fine work.

Those people whom I have mentioned by name in the book are some of the founder members and some of the technical staff, including test pilots, whom I frequently meet.

My wife has always encouraged me to continue writing this book when I felt like giving up; and my secretary, Ella Chapman, has tackled the typing with characteristic cheerfulness and efficiency. She has also done a mass of research in checking dates, names and facts.

I must thank Miss Constance Babington Smith, the authoress of *Evidence in Camera* and *Testing Time* for her helpful and kindly criticisms. And I should like to acknowledge my debt to Charles Gibbs-Smith, whose book *The Aeroplane—an Historical Survey* helped me greatly in obtaining facts and figures.

CONTENTS

ILLUSTRATIONS
Between pages 112–113

The motor cycle which I designed and which had some novel features: Note the unusual coiled finning on the cylinder.

My first aeroplane which flew. Frank Hearle starting the engine.

Louie, my first wife, stitching the covering for our first aeroplane in the workshop at Fulham.

The first de Havilland aeroplane which flew, photographed at Seven Barrows, Hampshire, where I learned to fly.

The first of my aeroplanes which flew, doing acceptance trials at Farnborough.

D.H.60 Gipsy Moth with sealed Gipsy engine, flown by Hubert Broad for twenty-four hours non-stop.

My three sons *(left to right)*, Peter, John and Geoffrey, discussing the tail of a Mosquito.

Peter de Havilland, Geoffrey Jnr., John, Hereward and Sir Geoffrey de Havilland.

Olivia de Havilland and Sir Geoffrey in Comet Cockpit.

Wild Animal Photography.

The D.H.98 Mosquito war machine, of which 7,781 were built.

The D.H.106, Comet 4, four Rolls-Royce Avon engines, with wing tanks for longer range.

MEDLEY

I HELD the handkerchief up to the wind and Hearle and I watched it anxiously. So long as it did not blow out more than four or five degrees from the vertical we knew it was all right. It hardly stirred in the light breeze. Flying conditions were ideal. We started up the four-cylinder engine and the fragile framework of our box kite shuddered because the balance of the engine was not too good. It seemed scarcely possible that this delicate assembly of timber, piano wire and doped fabric that I had designed and we had put together with our own hands could be persuaded into the air. And yet, several others had done this before us. Six years had passed since Wilbur and Orville Wright had left the ground at Kittyhawk after they had trained on gliders, but that epoch-making first flight was almost secret. The Wright Brothers' *Flyer* had a rather crude chain drive to the propellers, one chain being crossed to give opposite rotation. This worked well, but I thought a better mechanical job would be made by using bevel gearing, and we adopted this. The Wright Brothers had a weight and pulley launching gear, and it is highly probable that they had used this arrangement for launching their gliders when learning to fly. We fitted strong bicycle-type wheels for our landing gear.

I climbed carefully into the crude basket seat secured to the naked frame members and called down to Hearle: 'I'll taxi some way up the hill so as to get a good run down into wind.' Then I opened the throttle and lurched over the

13

turf up the slight incline until I was near the top and turned the machine round. It was a perfect winter's day in 1909. On one side Beacon Hill rose up eight hundred feet to the old Roman encampment at its summit, and on the other the ground fell towards the far older remains of Seven Barrows. Ahead of me and from the base of the slope down which I was about to race, the gently rolling Hampshire landscape spread into fields and copses. It was a good day and a good place to go flying, and I felt no premonition of danger.

The twin propellers behind me increased their revolutions. We had fined their pitch the day before in order to get more power and higher thrust. That was after I had said emphatically to Hearle, after doing hours of useless taxiing, 'Tomorrow we're going to make that aeroplane *do* something.' I was just as determined today.

For some yards the machine bumped and pitched about on the rough grass, increasing its speed as I opened the throttle wider and wider. I was travelling faster than ever before down the hill, and I knew I was near the safety limit. This was the moment, I was sure. I pulled back hard on the stick. The front went up at a steep angle as I climbed vertically, and I found myself looking up into the clear sky, while my weight on the seat seemed suddenly to have increased alarmingly.

There was no time to correct the error. Before I could thrust the stick forward again, I heard the sound of snapping woodwork around me. Still travelling forward at a fair speed I fell rapidly back to the ground and struck it heavily at the same time as the splintered wings and frame of the aircraft all around me. For some reason I was not knocked unconscious, and my first instinctive act was to stand up amongst the wreckage and wave to Hearle to show that I was all right. As a result I received a sharp and painful blow on the wrist, and sat down again. One of the propellers was still rotating gamely above my head.

The next thing I remember through my slight con-
cussion was Frank Hearle and my brother Hereward running up the hill. Behind them ran my father. He had hidden
behind the shed pleading that he could not stand the strain
of watching my first flight. He had, quite clearly, been
right, and as soon as he was assured that I was alive he
hastened home, speechless with shock.

*

This first brief flight had been made possible by the
generosity of my grandfather on my mother's side, Jason
Saunders, a most remarkable man who had a strong influence on the first twenty years or so of my life and who
can be considered, indirectly, to have been the originator
of all the de Havilland aerial activities. Jason Saunders
came from humble yeoman farmer stock on the outskirts
of Oxford, and had limited education and no special advantages as a young man. But he was a hard worker and
possessed of an uncommonly acute business sense. Many
years before I was born he had built up a thriving transport, removal and warehousing company in Oxford in
addition to a big farm at Medley. He was also politi-
cally and socially active, was an ardent Liberal, Mayor of
Oxford in 1876, and a devoted Freemason. As a young boy
I saw my grandfather as a thickset man of medium height
with white hair and grey moustache, blue-grey eyes and
ruddy cheeks. He usually looked rather severe, except in
the evenings when he would relax in a velvet smoking
jacket beside the fire, with a pipe or cigar and a glass of
whisky. With his growing affluence, Jason Saunders liked
to dress well, and I remember him at Medley during the
summer holidays when we used to stay there, striding
about in a 'square' bowler hat and with a walking stick,
and always with a horseshoe tie-pin carrying a fox's head
set in his stock tie. Grandfather knew and loved horses
and was a great hunting man. He even attempted to make

a horseman out of me on one of our visits. He gave me a lecture on the rudiments of riding, then put me on a pony to ride about the meadows. After a very quiet start and a short distance, the pony suddenly decided to return home. The wonderfully sharp hairpin turn threw me off, I was winded, and from that time have had no interest in horses.

Medley was as close to a self-sufficient farm as grandfather could make it, with the horse as the dominant figure, and with the timeless rural crafts practised at the highest level. It was characteristic of my grandfather, for example, that he made all the vans for his Oxford business as well as the farm wagons at Medley, from felling the timber off his own land to shrinking on the iron tyres and painting and lettering the finished vehicles. All this was done by blacksmith, carpenter and wheelwright in their own workshops set out round the pleasant manor yard. I knew all these men well, for whenever I was there I would be in and out of their shops, watching them at work and talking to them. There was the blacksmith, Cox, who had a fringe of grey whiskers and beard and wore a leather apron and cap, and his one-eyed assistant, Jack. Jack always wore a bowler hat above his black eye shade, and I never failed to be impressed by the skill with which he wielded the great two-handed sledge-hammer, aiming it with remarkable one-eyed accuracy. Harris, the general carpenter, also wore a bowler at work. He had a soft voice and a gentle round face, and was usually to be found knee-deep in sweet-scented wood shavings. Druid, the wheelwright with the long white beard, on the other hand, was usually rather irritable as he worked away, seemingly for ever shaping spokes for wagon wheels.

Everything at Medley Manor seemed well-ordered. The brougham in which we went to the City Church in High Street on Sundays shone like a black mirror outside, and inside was deeply upholstered in shiny black leather. The brougham had thin, solid rubber tyres, which were rare at that time, and accentuated the regular clop-clop of the horse's hooves. Medley has always been a place of nostalgia for me. In that brougham there was the faint scent of eau-de-Cologne, from Granny in her black seal-skin jacket, and this was mingled with the slightly musty scent of leather. I can still hear the musical notes of hammer on anvil, the hum of the chaff-cutter, and recapture the warm scents of the garden, the bed of violets, the earthy smell from the potting shed and the scent of peaches and nectarines from the hot walls which seemed to reflect the glow of perpetual sunshine. It was a heavenly place.

The house was very old and ivy-covered, and the large garden was enclosed by high white walls and there were masses of fruit trees of all kinds. In the centre of the garden was a large oval lily pond, its dark waters deep and rather frightening. All this was bounded on three sides by lovely meadows bordered by brooks, and it was in these meadows that I first became interested in butterflies and moths, an interest which increased as I became older and learnt more of their habits and life history. Across the home meadow stood a copse, wonderful and mystic to me, and from here came the oak, ash and poplar for the home workshops to be made into the wagons. Near the rickyard in a big old barn a steam engine and cutter turned the hay from many ricks into chaff for the animals. Besides the horses in the stables and fields, there were the chickens, ducks and guinea-fowl, the special responsibility of my grandmother, a very dear, gentle person, who took her full share of work on the farm and was always to be seen in a long black flounced dress with a lace cap on her silvery hair.

It was not until later that I realized fully what a sheltered and carefree life my mother, an only child, had led before her marriage, with a few close friends, plenty of servants and the gentle routine of visiting the poor and sick, going to market with her mother or for drives in the brougham, to come home to a little game of bezique in the evening; or perhaps running with the hounds at Foxcombe, or in later childhood attending the local Masonic Ball. As a boy at Medley I did not understand how ill-prepared she must have been for her marriage to my father, nor what a strong contrast life in an industrial town with a poor and eccentric parson must have been after the security and pastoral delights of Medley Manor.

*

I once found an old parchment in an attic amongst a pile of papers and letters. It was titled 'A Genealogy of the de Havillands'. As I was not highly interested, it was not seen again for many years but was sent to me on my father's death. I showed it to a cousin and she at once proposed making a careful search to bring the genealogy up to date because the original only went as far as 1840. She devoted most of her time to this end, and it was a true labour of love. She died only a year or so after completing it.

The Genealogy starts off with a 'Note': 'In a very ancient History of the conquest of England by William Duke of Normandy the name of De Havylland is mentioned as one of the Officers or Knights who accompanied the Conqueror.' There was, however, a letter amongst the pile of papers of more interest, and at least genuine. Headed 'Verdun, 27 May 1813' it is from Charles de Havilland addressed to his father 'Peter de Havilland, High Bailiff of the Island of Guernsey'. Charles was a prisoner of Napoleon in France. The letter is too long to quote in full but it starts: 'My dearest Father, It grieves me to the heart to find myself obliged to destroy all the hopes you had conceived . . . to get me those certificates to tell you they are scarcely any use in this country. . . . A French Admiral who has a son, a midshipman in England, tried to get him exchanged . . . but notwithstanding the hopes that had been given him . . . he received a very civil letter saying the Emperor would not hearken to any private exchange . . . Adieu best of Fathers, I wish I could embrace you all. Charles de Havilland.' This Charles was my great grandfather, and was born in 1786. He must have got away from France in the end, because he married when thirty-five and had a large family between 1821 and 1832. My grandfather on my father's side, whom I never met, was a clergyman and his brother was a general. There was an occasion when the parson and the general arranged to meet their wives at a railway station but the husbands did not turn up and were found much later bemused but happy in the bar of the local inn. My father's half-brother Walter, was the father of Olivia de Havilland and her sister Joan Fontaine.

I was born on July 27, 1882, in a village near High Wycombe, where my father was curate. My elder brother, Ivon, was already three. The first thing I can remember is my father letting off fireworks on the fifth of November and a ball of fire going over our house, an achievement that seemed to me of world-wide importance. My next memory is of our new house being built on the outskirts of Nuneaton, a small industrial town in the Midlands where my father had been appointed vicar. Here were born my sisters Ione and Gladys, and my younger brother Hereward, in that order. We lived here for the next fifteen years and through many a fretful financial crisis and outburst of tears from my poor harassed mother.

My father, Charles de Havilland, was a fine-looking man, but was handicapped by having a short left leg, and he had to wear a conspicuous big boot to compensate. I think he was always sensitive about this. He was educated at Merchant Taylors' School and from there went on to Oxford where he obtained his M.A. degree. He was considered to be a brilliant preacher. He was also unusually strict about the observance of the Sabbath, and on Sundays we were supposed to put away model engine catalogues and toys and read only 'suitable' books. We were also expected to go to church, preferably twice. There is no doubt that this discipline made me dislike Sundays for long afterwards. Father was really a kind man, but he did have what used to be called 'a hasty temper', and when this was aroused, sometimes on the smallest pretext, there were terrible outbursts of shouting accompanied by much arm-waving. There was an occasion, for example, when he was attempting to carve a tough leg of mutton and could make no impression with the knife. Suddenly he rose with a loud cry of anger and despair and flung the joint into the fireplace. Such scenes were not uncommon.

My father had two other weaknesses, one of which was often embarrassing, the other exasperating. He had a most strange attitude towards money matters, with a strongly held belief that well-off people should be glad to lend him money and not pester him for payment, and that tradesmen should not send in their bills, or if they did should not expect to be paid for a long time. This made for considerable awkwardness when we were sent on errands to shops in town and were told bluntly to pay our bills or get out. The ceaseless money troubles were the chief cause of the rows at home and of our poor mother's periods of depression and tearfulness. His other failing was his instinct for hoarding. When we later lived at Crux Easton, we had in the garden some fine William pear trees trained on the flint walls of the garden. Theirs was forbidden fruit; instead, when the fine big pears were ready for picking, my father would bring them into the house where they were carefully laid on shelves in his study 'to ripen'. They ripened but were never eaten. If anyone asked for a pear, the invariable answer was, 'They require a few more days'. Nothing more was heard of them until they were discovered, collapsed into a sodden mass and covered with mould. I don't think he ever ate one himself. He also kept Muscovy ducks, for no reason that we ever discovered, and their eggs, too, were laid out on the study shelves, apparently to ripen. Periodically the study shelves were cleared of pear pulp and rotten duck eggs.

It was in this study, so often surrounded by rotten pears and eggs, that my father worked away at the book that was going to make history, or at least to re-shape it. None of us was allowed to learn much of the details of this book, but it was supposed to be about the position of an important town or other locale in the Bible story which, he claimed, had been wrongly interpreted. He was certain that the commonly accepted geographical position was wrong by many hundreds of miles. When this error had been proved, in his book, it would cause the history of the East to be rewritten. His book would always be finished 'soon', but when he died many years later I made the pathetic discovery that it had scarcely been begun. My father's reasoning was always dogmatic, and nothing could persuade him that he was ever wrong. He actually disliked anything relating to mechanical or electrical matters, and certainly had no knowledge of them. But on one occasion I remember when we were suffering from an acute bout of dim electric lighting, my father had no doubt of the cause. 'I have found out why we get so little electric light,' he told my brother Ivon and me. 'In some rooms the light bulbs have been taken from their sockets, and this allows the electricity to stream out of the empty lamp holders.' And no explanations from us could disabuse him.

When he was not working on his great book, my father was usually to be found gardening, a hobby which gave him great pleasure. Wearing an alpaca jacket and black and white speckled boater hat, he would work hard for hours on end, and then stump indoors with an armful of vegetables enough for twenty people. He was curiously prodigal with his vegetables, but he never bothered with flowers; they were my mother's job. Gardening may well

21

have given him some release and escape from the cares and burdens of his domestic life and the constantly recurring financial crises. Considering his upbringing it is surprising that my father was not more eccentric. His mother had died when he was very young, and he was dragged up by an old nurse who had to look after the whole family. His father soon married again so he cannot have had much of a home life. Later in life I got to understand him better and was sorry for him when, after my mother died, he impulsively re-married and had an unhappy time with a hard and unsympathetic wife. When he was sixty-five he became seriously ill. I saw his doctor who said it was cancer and that it was incurable. It was difficult to persuade him to go to a nursing home as he had never been really ill before and dreaded any treatment. But eventually he had to go, and when I asked him if he was comfortable he said, 'It is peace and heaven and all the nurses are angels.'

The difficulties at home were not helped by the withering scorn which my parents' respective families felt for each other. My mother's family, the Saunders, looked upon the de Havillands as haughty, irresponsible and not quite honest, and were in turn looked down on as uneducated upstarts. The two families hardly ever met.

In Nuneaton's environment of anxiety, coupled with the burden of running the household and bringing up her children, it is scarcely surprising that my mother began to suffer increasingly from attacks of nerves followed by periods of exhaustion and depression. Naturally, she was a cheerful women with a nice sense of humour, a love of music and books and a genuine interest in Ivon's and my mechanical experiments. She gave all the time she could spare from the multitude of duties of a parson's wife to our care and happiness. But life at Nuneaton in the end proved too much for her, and my grandfather, who was constantly helping the family out of debt, bought my father an avowson at Crux Easton in Hampshire so that she could enjoy again the delights of a country life she had known as a child. But I doubt if she was any happier at Crux Easton than she had been at Nuneaton.

The stone house at Nuneaton had been built specially for us on three acres of ground, of which two were meadow. It seemed at first unpromising for children's games, but part of the garden had been the site of an old abbey, of which some of the ruins remained. These gave a certain sense of mystery to the place, and we made good use of them in our games. The meadows were bounded by a brook, and this later became the scene of our battles with the 'cads'. Class divisions were accepted without question in the 1890s, and it seemed perfectly normal to look upon the lower class children as 'cads' if only because this was the reflected view of our parents and their friends. These battles were harmless enough affairs, and they provided Ivon and me with an opportunity to exercise our mechanical ingenuity. For one combat we armed ourselves with a machine gun made by mounting a piece of one-inch gas pipe three feet long on our two-wheeled 'mail-cart'. When it was loaded with black gunpowder rammed down with wads of paper, it made a terrific roar when flame was applied to the touch hole. The 'cads' on the whole admired the noise it made and were not much intimidated; with reason, for the danger was far greater to us than it was to them. Clods of earth dipped in water, however, were the more usual ammunition. There was little real hatred, in fact, and we often played together when out of sight of the house. At the age of nine I even fell in love with one of the girl cads, and we got as far as exchanging bunches of flowers.

Another figure of importance in the garden was 'Bumunwhitething', the gardener, who acquired this name from the large posterior and white coat he often revealed when bending over the vegetables. A more proper nickname was 'Clench', from the manner in which he clenched his teeth when angry, although I am certain now that he had long ago lost all his teeth. Parker was very old and had fought in the Crimea. He had a muzzle-loading gun of great antiquity, and sometimes Ivon and I were allowed to try shooting out the flame of a lighted candle on the kitchen table with it, using percussion caps only of course.

For a time at Nuneaton, Ione, Gladys, Hereward and I were taught by a governess, while Ivon went to a dame school. Later I followed Ivon to the dame school, and then to the local grammar school as a day boy. Here I learnt for the first time to fear another person. The headmaster's name was Samuel, a small wizened man whom no one had ever seen smile, let alone laugh. I am certain that his great black moustache was grown only to terrify. Even his habit of returning from school or church in a sort of shuffling run was grotesque rather than funny. I hated him deeply, of course, and my hatred was if possible intensified when he caused me to commit my first crime. He took my form in history, and my history book was lost. To appear without it was impossible to contemplate. In desperation I stole half a crown out of a drawer at home in order to buy a replacement copy. I hope and think this was the only occasion when I wittingly committed a felony.

When I was about twelve I went as a boarder to a preparatory school in Rugby. Oakfield was a good school, and I learnt more there than anywhere else. I even enjoyed the games and for a short period achieved transient fame as a slow bowler. St. Edward's School, Oxford, was much less satisfactory. Today it enjoys a fine reputation, but in my time it suffered under a hard and unapproachable Warden who gave the whole place an unsatisfactory tone. I never cared for St. Edward's, although I could at least, by breaking bounds, walk across Port Meadow to beloved Medley.

During all my school years Medley meant more to me than any other place, and my grandfather remained the most important figure in my life. Medley provided me with almost all my early delights in natural history, and also in fishing, especially pike fishing. The pike at one time exercised a strange and almost sinister fascination over me, and this began among the brooks, all tributaries of the River Isis, among the meadows at Medley. I think my obsession for the pike began one day when my father—who rarely visited Medley—Ivon, and the groom, Odey, all went up the river as far as Godstow on a fishing expedition. I remember going to meet them on their return late in the evening to see if they had caught anything. They had. In the basket were two pike. Even more exciting than this was the news that Odey had been bitten in the thumb while taking the spinner and hook out of the fish's mouth. Breathlessly I asked, 'Did it bleed?' 'Yes, it did,' Ivon told me; and when I asked how much, he added, 'About an eggcup full.' I looked with awe at Odey's bandaged thumb, and knew this was the perfect end to a day's fishing. Bitten by a pike! From that time my interest in pike developed into an obsession. I read everything I could about pike, and listened to any exciting story about them I could persuade people to tell.

Pike are certainly sinister fish, and there are no other British fresh water fish like them. They live the solitary life of a killer, devouring at a swallow other fish, including their own species, water birds, full grown moorhens as well as chicks, frogs, voles and even other fish of their own size, killing themselves as well as their victim. One day when walking along the river margin I came to a long clump of reeds and heard the harsh chattering of reed-warblers which built there most years, their nests cleverly suspended amongst the reed stems. But the brooks held a greater fascination than birds' nests, and I veered off along a brook side and suddenly saw my first live pike. He was lying above the weed, quite motionless, the long, mottled, greenish body a wonderful camouflage against the water weeds. I knew those jaws contained rows of teeth with the longest all along the margin of the jaws, and needle sharp. I could not resist trying to touch the fish with a long hedge cutting, but just before the stick reached it, the pike shot away and disappeared. I strolled back to the house in the evening and heard the familiar call of the corncrake or landrail, whose nests I often found in the long grass at Medley.

One of the pike stories I heard, from my grandfather, told of a friend of his who would untie his bootlace, make a noose at one end, tieing the other to a stick cut from the hedge. Then he would slowly and skilfully lower the noose into the water and draw it gradually over the pike's body without touching it, then with a sudden upward flick draw the noose tight over the fish and pull it on to the grassy bank. I tried a variation of this unorthodox method by using a three-pronged pike hook and moving it slowly under the chin of the fish and then giving it an upward flick. I landed a number of pike of one or two pounds by this less skilful method.

More serious interests later put a stop to pike fishing, but it revived again when my son John and I were able to fish in a large private lake near Crux Easton. After the shallow brooks of my childhood, this was deep water fishing, and the excitement was the greater because we could look into the dark waters and imagine monsters of forty pounds lurking below. Even when the float plunged out of sight it was not possible to judge the size of the fish. We made several catches of from four to ten pounds. Late one perfect evening we were just packing up our gear when John said, 'I'll just have a last go'; and threw a good long cast far out into the lake, the roach making a big splash as it hit the water. Less than two minutes later John's float had gone under, and almost immediately he 'struck' hard, the reel screaming as a lot of line went out. 'It *feels* like a big one,' John said as he started to reel in, but there was rush after rush and a lot of line was still out. He reeled in again, calling out in a despairing voice, 'Damn, I think it's off and I'm tight in the weeds. I can't move it.' I took the rod from him and pulled steadily on the line. Suddenly the 'weeds' came to life and a lot more line screamed out. I handed the rod back to John and gradually the rushes got shorter and weaker until he was able to bring the fish near our boat. I was ready with the gaff, peering down into the dark water for a glimpse of him. A great, mottled, greenish form dimly appeared, still making weak rushes. At last I managed to slip the gaff into a gill opening and with a hand under the body, lifted the fish into the boat. It was a magnificent sight: a huge pike in perfect condition, which showed twenty-two and a half pounds on the spring balance. The reason this fish was so game and put up such a fine fight was, I believe, because it was hooked in the front part of the jaws, in the horny lips where no real injury was done nor any real pain caused. When a pike gets the bait and hooks down its throat it cannot fight much, and can usually be hauled in like a log. We propped its mouth open in order to guard against being badly hurt, and easily took out the hooks, and John was able to put his gloved hand far down its great jaws with their long sharp teeth. It had been such a perfect ending to an epic fight that we gladly returned our pike to its natural home, and although a little slow at first, it soon disappeared into the dark water.

*

Crux Easton is high up on the north Hampshire downs, only a few miles from Seven Barrows, and in the days when we moved there consisted of rectory, village school, church, farmhouse and less than a dozen scattered cottages. The views are magnificent, and it is so remote that it is hard to find any houses at all among the rolling downs and woods. Even today the lanes and woods still have the same atmosphere of remoteness and peace that I knew as a boy. I grew to love it as much as I always loved Medley. The Rectory at Crux Easton was large and rambling, with ten bedrooms and the usual inconveniences of one bathroom, septic tank drainage, pumped water from underground tanks that drew their supply from the roof and gutters, cooking on an old-fashioned range, and heating only by individual fires in rooms. These, of course, were very rare except in the sitting-room, and passages and bedrooms were perishingly cold in winter. My poor mother was often overwhelmed by trying to run this large and difficult house on little money and the minimum of servants, who were in any case constantly changing because of the Rectory's remoteness and the hardships of life there.

But if my mother found the new rectory as difficult and overwhelming as the old one, we enjoyed it much better than Nuneaton. The old part of the house, to which had been added a more recent wing, was reputed to be haunted, and although we never actually saw a ghost, we often heard mysterious noises. In winter we could explore the cellars, where the invariably empty wine bins were kept. In the summer there were the large garden and the outbuildings and the greenhouse with its great vine which reached right up the house walls and from which grapes could be picked from some of the bedroom windows. But it was the outbuilding housing the engine, dynamo and accumulators for the Rectory's electricity that provided Ivon and me with most interest.

I had developed from the earliest years I can remember an enthusiasm for engineering and mechanics which was to become no less absorbing than my love for natural history. Both have remained with me all my life. Even when I was at the little Dame school at Nuneaton I found it difficult to concentrate on any lessons that did not relate to my two enthusiasms. My brother Ivon, who was far ahead of me in theoretical and mathematical ability and later gave evidence of his brilliance in the advanced designs of motor-cars, was my tutor and collaborator, and for this reason alone a strong bond grew up between us. I looked on Ivon as being all-wise and the possessor of almost infinite knowledge of things mechanical and electrical. I think my first engine was a working model stationary steam engine, made in Germany and costing just one shilling. Ivon was more ambitious and sent for castings for a better type of engine, which cost one and sixpence. The fact that we had none of the necessary tools to complete the engine in no way diminished our enthusiasm. Later on, when Ivon was at Rugby, he returned one holiday with a fine model cylinder and valve gear already machined. From our precious model engine catalogue we bought item by item the required parts, improvising others, until we possessed the complete set to finish the engine. We had to save up for a long time for the boiler and its fittings, however, and, impatient to see if it would work, we tried blowing hard down the steam pipe at least to achieve some motion. By nearly bursting our lungs we got the engine turning over fairly fast and so were able to adjust the valve gear for the best setting. Later we got the boiler as a combined Christmas present and soon had it mounted and the connections made. The great day arrived for the trial run, and the engine worked well. This event became a small but definite milestone in our progress.

Over the years there were more engines and experiments than I can possibly remember. There was, for example, the marine steam engine which I used to power a boat I made in the school workshops. I was a long time on this job and it became something of a joke at school. But when I finally launched it, it worked very well and most impressively, and my standing rose accordingly. Ivon and I also built an elaborate railway layout in the Parish Room in the garden and ran our own locomotives on it. There was always something like this going on.

The most interesting, prolonged and expensive experiments in which Ivon and I indulged were with the electrical plant at Crux Easton. We went there as an advance party in 1896 before the family moved in, staying at a nearby farm, in order to equip our new house with electricity. Subsidized, as usual by our grandfather, we bought the necessary wire and fittings and laid these without great difficulty, although electric lighting was still uncommon in private houses at that time. Ivon had, however, under-estimated the cost of the operation and we had to make do with a cheap small paraffin oil engine and fifty-volt dynamo for the power equipment. Both these were unsatisfactory, and the most light we got from the dynamo was a terrific sparking from the brushes. After some abortive experimental work, we had to confess ourselves defeated. 'To make sure, we had better get a steam engine and boiler and a first class dynamo,' Ivon decided. These were eventually installed, an excellent Brush Electrical Company dynamo, a boiler that demanded constant stoking and adjustment of the water level, and engine that was reliable enough to give us real electric light for a while. I derived enormous pleasure from attending to the needs of this machinery, but when I left for boarding school no one else was prepared to carry on with the dirty and strenuous work. So boiler and engine were again sold and a new oil engine, doubtless paid for by grandfather, took their place. This engine 'knocked' so badly when it got hot that it, too, had to go. But the two-cylinder second-hand petrol engine that followed gave even more trouble and did less running than all its predecessors put together. By now a certain amount of bad feeling was developing, and Ivon and I, with every justification, were accused of frivolous experimentation. This succession of power units had certainly been appallingly expensive, but we had at least gained a great deal of pleasure and practical experience from them. Success was finally achieved with a

Crossley oil engine which worked faultlessly, gave us constant electric light and required little attention.

*

After leaving St. Edward's at seventeen I went to a rectory near Gloucester where the parson tried to coach a few boys, but I think his methods, anyhow, in my case, were quite useless. It was assumed at home that I should follow my father by entering the Church, but when I considered the matter seriously I realized that all my interests centred on mechanical engineering, especially those dealing with motor-car design, something relatively new and exciting. Motor-cars were still a rare sight at the turn of the century in the country, but abetted by Ivon, I absorbed all the information I could find about them. In Gloucester the owners of a large cycle shop had daringly bought two $3\frac{1}{2}$-h.p. Benz cars, and a friend and I saved up and hired one, with a driver, to take us to Newbury at the end of term. It was the first time I had been in a motor-car, and it was a great adventure. We had to help the car up Birdlip Hill as the leather transmission belts slipped on their pulleys, but after reaching the top we careered along the level stretches at anything up to 15 m.p.h. We eventually arrived at Newbury feeling like returning explorers and surrounded by a crowd of excited sightseers.

We had scarcely, in the popular phrase, annihilated space. But after that short drive I knew that my future life lay in the world of mechanical travel. The fascination of independently powered and swift transportation from place to place that was to seize so many of the young of my generation had gained a hold which was never to relax through all my working life.

CHAPTER TWO

CRYSTAL PALACE DAYS

S EVERAL months after that first exciting ride in the
Benz, we bought our first motor-car. Very few other
people had one as early as that, and it must have been as a
result of pressure from Ivon and me—and doubtless
financed by grandfather. It was a two-year-old Panhard-
Levasseur, a 6-h.p. twin-cylinder machine with large
diameter rear wheels shod with rubber solid tyres, and
smaller front wheels with pneumatic tyres which were
always bursting. Even in its natural open state it was very
high off the ground, but for the comfort of the four rear
passengers a great removable box with glass windows
could be fitted on top, when the Panhard assumed the
appearance of a conservatory set up on end. Even without
this addition the centre of gravity was very high, but with
the 'hard top' in place this car was one of the most unstable ever built, as my father discovered to his cost before
we even got it home for the first time from London. A
driver supplied by the agents for the journey was at the
controls alongside Ivon at the time when a pony crossed
the road at dusk right in front of them. The slightest
departure from a steady straight line was almost certain to
lead to trouble, and in this case the Panhard turned over
immediately on to the grass verge. Fortunately father was
seen to emerge from the wreckage of broken glass, tools,
and spare tins of oil and petrol without harm and still
clutching his top hat, and next day the Panhard was turned

over to the nearest coachbuilder, Hamilton of Highclere, for repairs.

Hamilton's family had been coachbuilders for generations. He was a remarkably striking and handsome man whom we all liked. This was as well, for now that we were motor-car owners we were obviously going to see much more of him. It also seemed somehow appropriate that with his finely chiselled features and long black beard he should look like one of the Apostles. He certainly needed saintly patience as far as the Panhard and the de Havillands were concerned. I was driving him back to Highclere one day when something went wrong and the car set off at a tangent towards the ditch. I was quite unable to correct the swerve and jammed on the brakes as we struck the verge. Hamilton disappeared from the passenger seat beside me, and the next I saw of him he was sitting in the hedge facing me, apparently quite unruffled although with his heavy beard as well as dark goggles it was difficult to judge his expression. With the calmness of Saint Paul leaving the prison at Philippi, he disentangled himself, walked unhurriedly back to the Panhard and at once identified the cause of the trouble in a broken front spring.

Before Ivon and I left home we determined to teach my sister Ione and, if possible, our mother how to drive the Panhard. From the moment you tried to swing the starting handle the car demanded uncommon strength, skill and courage. The gear change was very tricky, the rack-and-pinion steering was always trying to take charge and sent up to your wrists every shock from the rough and stony road surface. There was of course no windshield nor cover of any sort for the driving compartment. Rather to my surprise, they both won their battles with the Panhard, and we left with the reasonable certainty that they would remain mobile and unharmed.

Like the electric lighting at Crux Easton, the car was made to suffer constant attention and experimental work from Ivon and me. With Hamilton's help we lengthened the chassis frame in an effort to give it greater stability, and Ivon fitted electric ignition in place of the deadly tubes, which required to be heated red hot by a small bunsen flame fed by petrol before the engine could be started.

I have described this old Panhard car in some detail because I am sure it was not only an invaluable 'test-bed' for Ivon and me, but finally confirmed our determination to go into one branch or another of creative engineering. It had to go in the end, of course, to be replaced by the pony and trap which our father understandably preferred, but for Ivon and me it was as much the beginning of a new era as it was for our father the closing of an unhappy experiment. It was not long before we were hard at work on our own car, and it was to be no ordinary car. It was to be a steam car and a racer. The newspaper magnate, Gordon-Bennett, had a lot to do with making motor racing popular in this country, and it was for one of the annual events bearing his name that our steam racer was to be built—and of course to win. The French Serpollet and American Stanley and Locomobile steam cars had done very well in short races, and we were certain that we could build one that would sweep the board. Naturally, money was the first consideration, but by skilful persuasion Ivon managed to obtain the backing of a wealthy man who was convinced that we were potential world-beaters. In a remarkably short time, and with the headlong enthusiasm of youth and ignorance, the large stable at Crux Easton was turned into a workshop and installed with two lathes, planing machine, drilling machine and an oil engine for power. For some months this became the centre of our world. We even bought a Locomobile steam car to see how it worked, and to get steam driving experience. The working knowledge we gained was negligible, the driving experience up and down the drive, with the most elementary brakes, often nearly fatal.

Ivon always worked with daemoniacal speed and energy, and never considered anything but the job in hand. I did my best to match his pace, with the result that in a surprisingly short time we had completed our steam racer's chassis, springs and steering. Road wheels were in place, and we were well on with the three-cylinder engine. Then, inevitably, the money ran out, and the de Havilland world champion racing car, that was to have won the Gordon-Bennett Cup and set up international records, had to be abandoned. It was heart-breaking after all our work to have our hopes dashed and to have nothing more than this pathetic skeleton to show for them. It was an expensive tragedy, of course, but it was a memorable warning to both of us of the dangers and difficulties in estimating time and cost of new experimental work. Right up to this present day, even the largest and best managed firms still make this same mistake when it comes to preparing a prototype.

So we went to the 1903 Gordon-Bennett races in Ireland as spectators instead of winning driver and mechanic and had to be content with experiencing vicariously the thrills of hurling the monsters of the time round the dusty roads outside Dublin. I remember that Jenatzy won on a 60-h.p. Mercedes and that he was considerably disappointed, after the emotional and excitable celebrations that greeted winning drivers on the Continent, at his reception at the finish. The English spectators were hoping that their hero, Edge, would win; and the Irish took no notice whatever of the proceedings, except to double their charges for everything.

During this period of motor activity at Crux Easton, Ivon had already set out on his engineering career. He had earlier shown an exceptional interest, and skill, in electrical engineering. Besides the wiring of our own house, he had taken great interest in the more elaborate electrical system at Rugby. In fact, he spent far more time in the

power house than he did in the classroom, although he
was a natural first-class mathematician. His vocation was
never in any doubt, and on leaving Rugby he went as
student apprentice to the Brush Electrical Engineering
Company at Loughborough. After passing out of there, he
got his first job at the Oxford Electric Light Company,
living with our grandparents at Medley. Later, his exceptional ability gave him a more important post with a consulting engineer in London. It was already clear, I think,
that Ivon was capable of doing really important work in the
electrical field, and his early enthusiasm never dimmed for
a moment. His only real danger was in working himself
out. He was never a robust young man, and he seemed
incapable of holding himself back. In London he worked
far too long hours. The result was inevitable. His health
broke down, he was found to have tuberculosis, and had to
go away for a year to a sanatorium in Norfolk, followed
by a long convalescence at Crux Easton. It was clear to
everyone, except perhaps to Ivon himself, that he would
have to learn to slow his pace in the future.

In 1900, some three years before Ivon's breakdown, I
had begun my training at the Crystal Palace Engineering
School. At first I lived with a family in Sydenham, but soon
joined up with another student in sharing digs. The great
iron and glass structure of the Crystal Palace had originally
been part of the Great Exhibition of 1851 in Hyde Park.
Re-erected at Sydenham, it was a conspicuous landmark
for nearly a hundred years until destroyed by fire before
the last war. It was the South Tower that housed the
Engineering School. In this were drawing office, pattern
shop, machine and fitting shops, electrical section and
three civil engineering sections. The methods employed
in the machine and fitting shops were archaic even for
those days, but I could at least learn the rudiments of
machining and fitting. The civil engineering sections were
more up to date, but I was never interested in large struc-

tures like dams and bridges. I liked the work in the drawing office and the workshops better than attending lectures, and after passing through the various sections, had one term in civil engineering. Most students schemed to get on this course during the summer term because we used to go surveying in the extensive Palace grounds among the woods and lakes. This nearly always ended with the two surveying parties starting a battle, ranging rods being used as spears, mud being flung from the lake shores, and by careful manœuvring, forcing the enemy into the water.

We all had a free pass into the Palace itself, and many of us spent the evenings there. There was entertainment for every taste, including a roller skating rink, variety theatre (best seats one and sixpence), a good library, a small zoo, organ recitals, choir festivals, performing fleas, dozens of minor side-shows and, in the summer, Brock's famous firework shows in the grounds.

Students could take an extra term in any section of the school to do some special work, and I took mine in the machine shop to build a motor cycle engine, rated at one and a half horsepower. Full details and drawings of this engine were given in an excellent magazine called 'The English Mechanic', and the castings and forgings could be bought in London. Making this engine was not only absorbing work that I really enjoyed, but was valuable practical experience. While building the engine I got friendly with a little man named Harris who had a small, combined bicycle and shoemaker's shop quite near our digs in Norwood. He never seemed to stop working, and was usually mending shoes up to eleven o'clock at night and repairing bicycles during the day. I was very sorry for him because he was often suffering from a black eye given him by his drunken wife. He had married a second time, and the two children by his first marriage had a terrible time from their stepmother. A poor thin little girl of about eight or nine, always in rags, was made to scrub the floors on hands and knees for most of the day. She was cursed all the time by her stepmother, and when one day I saw her beaten about the face and head I thought it time to write to the N.S.P.C.C. After that things improved.

I gave Harris the job of building a bicycle to take my engine. As motor cycles were still uncommon the components were not easy to get, so we decided to use 'tandem' parts and 'tandem' tyres. In 1902 most motor cycles had pedals and chain for starting and for helping up hills by pedalling. Transmission from the engine was by a leather belt to a large diameter vee pulley clipped to the spokes of the rear wheel. This was standard practice. The belt was a constant source of trouble, slipping in rainy weather and often failing at the joint or fastening, until rubber-canvas belts later came into use.

I did the final assembly of the engine and tank and bicycle at Crux Easton, but there was delay in getting a suitable belt. There was great excitement about the first test, and in desperation I got hold of a piece of tarred rope to use as a temporary belt. There was a rather rough, flinty lane leading to the rectory at Crux Easton. I wheeled the cycle to the top of the lane and started down the slope. The tarred rope quickly stretched and fell off, the brakes failed to stop the rush down the slope, and as the lane ended in the churchyard wall I leapt off 'under speed' as the lesser of the two evils. I hurt myself quite badly, with deep gashes in the knee and hand landing on the sharp flints. While out of action I was able to get a leather belt, and the next tests were more successful and improved each time.

Now I really felt as if I was getting somewhere. I was proud of my first motor bicycle in spite of its crudeness, and got enjoyment from the planning of journeys which, by modern standards, must have been pure agony. Any sort of springing was unknown, the tyres were small and unreliable, saddles small and harsh, and the frames were high. Skidding was an accepted hazard. But my pride

38

would not allow me to travel other than by motor cycle, and the journeys between Crux Easton and the Crystal Palace provided many adventures.

On one journey to London misfiring became so bad that I had to stop on the Bath Road for an investigation. Electric ignition was by 'trembler' coil and a make and break commutator on the camshaft, current being supplied from a dry battery. The sheet metal blade of the contact breaker was not making proper contact on the commutator, and in bending it for better contact it fractured. I had no spare, and vaguely looked along the roadside in the hope of finding a piece of wire that could be used temporarily. I eventually found a hairpin on the edge of the path. After cleaning, it was fitted with two prongs bearing on the commutator. The engine started and ran with less misfiring than before, but to make sure I examined the 'surface' or 'wick' carburetter, the body of which was a half-pound tobacco tin. The principle on which it worked was air drawn by the engine through a wick surrounding a gauze tube which stood in about an inch of petrol in the tobacco tin and became saturated. The level of petrol was controlled on the 'bird fountain' principle. I found that the wick—a portion of a discarded woollen sock—was torn, but soon tied it up with rag. The tobacco maker's name, stamped on the top of the tin, was discreetly covered by a good film of solder. I arrived at the Crystal Palace without further trouble. The hairpin did good service for many days. I gained a lot of useful experience from this sort of mishap.

In 1900 The Automobile Club's 1,000-mile Motor-Car Trial ended at the Crystal Palace. The cars were on show and gave trial runs in the grounds. Amongst the early enthusiasts was the Hon. C. S. Rolls; he was driving a Panhard car, and a few years later his name became famous coupled with that of Royce. I had a wonderful time examining in detail everything that could be seen in Daimler,

Panhard, Mors, Decauville, De Dion, Renault and other cars that became famous.

Theoretical work was less to my taste. I cannot remember ever passing an exam, and one of the only two prizes I ever received was for a paper I read in 1902 entitled 'The Motor-Car'. I still have the paper, and today it makes quaint reading. It ends with a daring look ahead—'Motorcars are becoming more familiar objects every day, and the time is not far distant when they will be as common as, if not more so, than horse-drawn vehicles are today.' At this time a motor-car was a fairly rare sight, and on my earliest motor cycle rides to London I seldom saw more than three or four cars during the whole journey of some sixty miles.

I learned a lot at the Palace and was sorry to leave; it had been a rewarding and happy three years. After a short holiday I entered the engineering works of Willans and Robinson at Rugby as student apprentice, a firm famous for high precision standards in the manufacture of Willans's central valve, single-acting steam engines, used at one time almost universally in electric generating stations. Later the firm made large gas engines and steam turbines and I gained a lot of useful and varied practical experience. Life here, as at the school, was good, with few cares or responsibilities, but I greatly missed all those varied evening entertainments at the Crystal Palace. Social life at Rugby consisted of visits to other students' digs for cards, beer, talk and occasional parties. We also visited the more lively towns like Birmingham, Leicester and Coventry in the evenings. But it wasn't the same thing at all.

However that was of little importance compared with my work. The more deeply involved I became in mechanical engineering, the more I realized that it was the one thing that mattered in my life and that no other career would have satisfied me. For instance I became passionately interested in my first real motor cycle engine. This one was entirely of my own design, one I had been thinking about for a long time. The engine was 450 c.c., which was large for that time, and it had an outside flywheel, mechanical inlet valve and various other novel features. The drawings were made in the digs in the evenings, and I did the machining and fitting in the works. A bicycle frame to take the new engine had to be made, and I wrote to the Superintendent of the Electrical Section at the Crystal Palace who was a keen cyclist and whose spare-time hobby was building very high grade hand built bicycles, in small numbers. He was willing to do the job, and I sent him rough drawings with dimensions. There would be no chain and pedal gear because the engine was of fairly high power. Frames were still high, for no good reason, and springing, even for front wheels, had not arrived. The bicycle was sent by train and I fitted the engine, tank and accessories in our workshop. The first few trial runs seemed very successful, but mechanical trouble soon developed. The outside flywheel was fitted on the tapered end of the shaft with the usual type of key. But before long the flywheel was running slightly out of true and on investigating it I found that the key had sheared its way nearly half-way round the shaft. A deeper keyway was tried with no better results. I had to machine a new crankshaft and flywheel, and this time the taper was made far finer, about one in ten, and no key was fitted. By using a long spanner on the nut and jamming the flywheel hard on the taper there was no slipping and no more trouble. Footrests were fitted instead of pedals, and it quickly became natural to put one's left foot on the flywheel to act as a brake. This was very efficient, but ruinous to the soles of my left shoes.

In spite of the crude braking mechanism, that motor bicycle was quite revolutionary for its time, and I believe the success of a design that was entirely my own was a great fillip to my self-confidence. Eventually my beloved bicycle was handed over to my younger brother, Hereward, who made good use of it for many years. I never knew what finally happened to it, but would be overjoyed to see it again, as I do sometimes in dreams. Later on, when I was hard up, I sold the drawings and patterns of the engine to two student friends for five pounds, and they eventually formed the very successful Blackburne motor cycle concern based on this engine and its development.

During my last six months at Willans I was given the job of testing their first petrol engine. This was very pleasant and exciting work, but Willans was a conservative firm and many members of the staff looked on internal combustion engines as nasty toys unfit to live in the same shop with Willans's steam engines.

My highest ambition at this time was to get a job in the drawing office of a motor-car firm, and in 1905 I joined the Wolseley Tool and Motor-Car Company at Adderley Park, Birmingham, as a thirty-shilling-a-week draughtsman. At that time there were important administrative changes going on at Wolseleys. The Managing Director was Herbert Austin, but now another man appeared. John Siddeley was equally able and ambitious, and it at once became clear that there wasn't room for both of them there. So Austin left and founded the Austin Motor Company, later becoming Lord Austin. He also became a millionaire, mainly through the success of the Austin Seven. This was entirely Austin's own idea, pushed through against the opposition of some of his staff and enabling him to take a personal 'rake off' of one pound per car. I cannot say I knew Austin as I was only a junior draughtsman, but I remember him coming round one day to look at the drawing boards and stopping at the man next to me who was the car body designer. Austin was very outspoken. He studied the body design and exploded: 'The rear of that body reminds me of a thing I keep under the bed. Tear it up and start again, and don't make it look so much like a damn'd po.'

The Wolseley cars of those days had horizontal engines driving a shaft in the gearbox by a single chain, and chains from the gearbox countershaft to the back wheels. Available in two-cylinder and also four-cylinder models, they were well made and reliable but noisy. There was also a smaller car with single-cylinder vertical engine, and I believe this car more or less marked the end of the horizontal engine at Wolseleys.

After a few months of making necessary but highly uninteresting general arrangement drawings, I was given small design jobs. But these were little more inspiring, and I found myself becoming restless. The work at Wolseleys was not my only reason. I did not like Birmingham which always seemed to me like an overgrown Nuneaton. I found digs at Small Heath and walked the two miles to work in the morning and back in the evening, lunching in the staff canteen. I think I was probably shy and diffident at that time, and the lack of friends made me feel lonely and rather miserable. The one friend I did make, after a long time, was the owner of a motor cycle shop near my digs. We had much in common. He was a good practical engineer and had invented and patented several ideas for the improvement of motor cycles, a front wheel springing method and other things which were not only new but good. Later on I made other friends through my week-end motor cycling, and we joined up and went for long rides through the Warwickshire countryside together, sometimes ending up at pubs or the music hall in the evening.

After six months or so at Wolseleys I felt happier and less lonely, but remained dissatisfied with the work. In spite of my youth, I wanted to create and be my own master. I already felt capable of doing really useful original work, but instead here I was doing uncongenial or dull jobs under harsh orders and a harsh régime. After sticking it for about a year, I determined to go. I had no idea where I would go or exactly what I would do. All I knew for certain was that I had to be my own master and do exciting creative work. Whatever it was, I felt sure I could make a success of it.

*

After a long convalescence at Crux Easton, Ivon had started work again, at the Daimler Motor Company, where, as designer and engineer he made some notable improvements to the cars then in production. But after eighteen months in Coventry he met an old Rugby school-friend, Guy Knowles, who had helped form the successful firm of Legros and Knowles. Ivon was offered the job of chief designer. It was a post he accepted with delight, for he now had a free hand to create an entirely new design and put into effect some of the ideas he had been thinking out for many years. The result was the Iris car of 1905, a most impressive motor that included many novel features in its specification. At the time of the Motor Show at which it first appeared I had just left Wolseleys, and was staying at home, temporarily unemployed. So when Ivon asked me to come up to London to help on the Iris stand I jumped at the chance. In the big hall at Olympia, it was a great moment when the crowds gathered round the stand, admiring the first tangible proof of Ivon's skill and imagination, the first fruit of the years we had studied and experimented together, from those first elementary model steam engines at Nuneaton to the abortive steam racer at Crux Easton. I had always been certain that he would achieve success, and eventually fame, as an engineer.

Ivon himself was unable to share the excitement at Olympia as he had been laid up with a chill. This was bad luck, and before returning home I called in at his house at Acton to console him with a report of the good reception his car had received. We talked of his work and his plans for the future, and when I left him I think he was in a more cheerful frame of mind. A few nights later I had a frightening dream. Ivon seemed to be lying helpless on the floor of my room, unable to move, while I was unable to help him. I awoke frightened and distressed and, for the first time in my life, lit a candle and left it burning beside me. When my mother came in the morning to wake me as usual, she saw the burnt out stub of the candle and asked me what had happened.

'I dreamt about Ivon last night,' I told her. 'It was a rather horrible and frightening dream—a nightmare really.' She consoled me and tried to cheer me up, and I had to confess that it seemed much less dreadful in the morning sunshine. My mother was to visit Medley that day, and later in the morning my sister Ione and I set out for the station with her to see her off. Half-way there we met the postman, who hailed us, waving a telegram.

'I was just on my way to you with this,' he told us. 'I hope it's not bad news.'

My mother's first words on reading it were: 'Your dream!' Ivon had died suddenly in the night. His chill had developed into serious influenza, which, irritated by the weakness caused by overwork, had ended in tragedy. Perhaps there was some other emotional trouble which contributed, but we never knew.

The sudden sense of loss I felt was overwhelming. Somebody on whom I had depended, for whom I had a deep affection, had been snatched away from me, almost overnight. There had always been a deep understanding between Ivon and me, and any future life without him seemed, for the present, unthinkable. I tried to put his death out of my mind and carry on as usual, but at first it was impossible, and for some years I had more strange dreams about him, in which he came back, but was secretive and strange before returning to an unknown place, lost to me again.

CHAPTER THREE

THE CHALLENGE

WHEN I was still very young two things happened to me that can, I think, now be seen as presages of the interest that was to engross me for the rest of my life. I had a model parachute from a Christmas cracker which I used to throw out of the highest window, watching it float gently to the ground. One day when I launched it a miracle happened. Instead of falling delicately to the earth, it started to rise, and went on rising until it passed over the stables in the yard. This was, of course, due to a local up-current of air, but even then seemed to have some special significance. At about the same time as this mysterious event, Ivon and I happened to be looking out of the same window listening to the sounds of a fête a mile away in Nuneaton. It was a beautiful summer's afternoon, and we could imagine the scene of colour and gaiety as we heard the vigorous music of a brass band floating towards us. Suddenly a great balloon rose up from the town, climbing steadily and fast and high into the sky. Fascinated, we watched it until it finally disappeared in the far distance and at a great height.

Neither Ivon nor I ever forgot that balloon, and even when our time and interest were absorbed by the motor-car and our plans to build one ourselves, we would talk occasionally about flying and the practicability of man one day conquering the air. We favoured the principle of vertical lift, and in this we were certainly inspired by one of our favourite books, Jules Verne's *Clipper of the Clouds*. The Clipper employed a dozen or more vertical fans, and in our enthusiasm we made numerous drawings and got as far as writing to the makers of electric fans to ask about the thrust and horsepower required. Meanwhile, other maturer and more experienced minds than ours were already at work, stimulated by the developing reliability of the internal combustion engine, which gave equal power with far less weight than the steam engine. For some reason Hiram Maxim, the most advanced experimenter in Britain and the inventor of the Maxim gun, favoured two steam engines and a boiler of amazing lightness and great ingenuity, as motive power. I was twelve when he was carrying out the trials with his extraordinary machine laid on rails in Baldwyn's Park in Kent, and eagerly read about them at the time. My friend and co-director, C. C. Walker, did better than this, though, and actually went on board for a test. He can confirm that the upper guard rails to prevent the machine from taking off were distorted, so proving that it had lifted. The world heard little about the early exploits of the Wright Brothers, but by 1906 or 1907 word began to filter through to people who were interested in such things that men like Santos-Dumont, Blériot, Voisin, Pelterie and Farman in France, and Cody, Roe and Dunne in England, were meeting with success and were actually making short hops.

The year 1908, when Wilbur Wright brought his machine to France and demonstrated it at Le Mans, marked the turning point for me, away from cars and towards the heavier-than-air craft. I read eagerly about Wright's astonishing displays at Le Mans in August, which were far ahead of anything achieved in Europe, and knew at once that, though I might never have seen an aircraft in the air, this was the machine to which I was prepared to give my life. My experience of the motor industry had so far been rather disappointing, and here was something new that inspired me with excitement. I was seized with an ambition to design and build my own aeroplane and engine and nothing was going to hold me back.

I sometimes wonder how many times my grandfather came to the rescue of the de Havillands in the last twenty or so years of his life. We were as poor as ever and my father was still subject to the old financial crises of my childhood, although perhaps on a reduced scale. Certainly I could hope for no backing from that quarter, nor were any other of our relatives likely to be able or willing to help. My mind turned automatically to Jason Saunders. It was a long shot, but he might help. He was an old man now, and had been suffering so badly from bronchitis at Medley that he and my grandmother had had to move to another large house in Oxford to get away from the dampness and river fog. But I knew his mind was as lively as ever and that he had avoided the common prejudices of old age. At least he would listen to me with sympathy.

I called on him at once. It was in the evening and he was in the sitting-room, wearing his usual smoking jacket. He had a long cigar alight, and beside him there was a whisky decanter and glass on a silver tray. He greeted me and at once began to talk with all his old energy and enthusiasm. 'There's talk about having some of these motor buses in Oxford and doing away with the horse trams. I had a lot to do with starting the trams years ago, and I'll be sorry to see them go, but I suppose we've always got to change. No use trying to hold things back. A man named Morris who used to have a motor cycle shop in Oxford is very keen on having motor buses,' he added, referring to the man who later became Lord Nuffield. He knew that at that time I was working on buses myself, and asked what I thought.

'They'll have to come to Oxford one day,' I said in agreement, and, taking this as my cue, went on rapidly, 'But I've now got a far greater interest than buses. It's flying. You remember we talked once or twice about aeroplanes. That's what I want to get into now. In fact I'm so keen to build one and fly that I'm trying to find someone to put up the money. But it's not going to be easy.'

My grandfather looked at me in silence for some seconds. At last he asked me, 'You really think you know enough about it to build a flying machine?'

At least he was showing some interest. This was no time for any doubts or show of modesty. I said emphatically, 'Yes, I'm certain I do, and I've an overwhelming desire to fly.'

There was another silence while my grandfather gave undivided attention to the length of ash hanging precariously to the end of his cigar. 'I intended leaving you a thousand pounds,' he said to me at last, 'but if you prefer to have it now you can. But there will be no more later on.'

I was so shocked by this sudden and exciting news that I hardly knew what to say. But I did manage to thank him, probably quite inadequately, before I left, my mind already hard at work dreaming and planning the future.

The next time I saw my grandfather he was ill in bed with bronchitis, and it was obvious that he was weakening. He recovered sufficiently to get about on fine days, and my mother went to see him. She had only been there a short time when she was taken very ill, I think with peritonitis. She died a few days later. My grandfather did not live long after this shock, but I was glad to feel that he had lived to see the beginning of the success that was due to his generous help at a critical time. He died in 1911. My grandmother lived on for nearly two years and stayed in the same big house, but with the loss of the dominant personality of my grandfather she seemed to lose her vitality and interest in life. My sister Ione went to live with her in her loneliness, but found it very hard going, for nothing she did was right, and she was forced to leave because our grandmother made it clear she wished to live alone. She soon declined physically and mentally, and then Ione returned and was with her at the end.

*

I had not been bluffing my grandfather when I told him that I was sure I could build an aeroplane. I had no doubts on that score; and I was equally certain that I should be able to teach myself to fly in it. What was far less certain was what would happen after I had done this, but I don't think I ever seriously considered this.

At that time it was difficult to see any practical use in flying, either military or civil. But all that was in the future, and would sort itself out. I was concerned only with the challenge that had now, quite suddenly, presented itself. All I was interested in was to start work at once, designing and building an aeroplane, and then flying it.

While working at Walthamstow I had met a young man named Frank Hearle. He was a tall and good-looking Cornishman who had served his apprenticeship with a marine engineering firm at Falmouth. Hearle is that rare sort of man who is at once liked and trusted by everyone, and we had become firm friends. It was obviously necessary to have some practical as well as financial help to build an aeroplane, and my obvious choice was Hearle, who was doing uncongenial work in the machine and fitting shops at the bus garage at Dalston. So the first thing I did after returning from my visit to Oxford was to go round to Hearle's digs and tell him the exciting news.

'I'm going to start straight away making drawings for an aeroplane engine,' I said, 'and while it is being made I'll begin work on the airframe. Will you come and help?'

Hearle gave me a look of pleased surprise and said, 'I'd love to. Can you tell me more about it? I'm not keen on spending much more time standing in a pit under the sump of a bus engine trying to *file* the worn crankpins to make them a bit more round.'

I told him I thought this new project might be a little more exciting. 'But I ought to warn you that I can't pay you much because the money is going to be tight. What are you getting now?'

'Ninepence-halfpenny an hour. That works out at about two pounds ten a week, but I can quite easily manage on less.'

When Frank Hearle moved into a flat in Kensington with me, in 1907, with my sister Ione to keep house for us, and helped to build the first de Havilland aeroplane at thirty-five shillings a week, there began a close business and personal relationship that has lasted to this day. Frank not only became an engineer of great practical experience, but developed high administrative and business ability, and became company chairman and managing director. He always had a natural and precious gift of creating goodwill and friendly co-operation wherever he went. The arrangement at Kensington worked well and was a happy one. I had always been fond of Ione—or 'Onie' as she was always called—in spite of the hot arguments we often had. She seemed to like taking an opposite point of view just to start an argument, or to be different. She could be maddening and exasperating and we often shouted at each other, but she had a delightful sense of humour and was always an entertaining companion. Her ideas always tended towards the extreme, and in politics she was more to the Left than the most rabid Labourite. She was also very public spirited, being responsible in later years for starting the public library at Bushey Heath and for much of the welfare work for old people in that district. Onie was an ardent and clever gardener and ran a house well and efficiently. It was not long before Frank fell in love with her, and later they married and lived happily together until her untimely death in 1953. Frank and Onie had one son, Patrick, who works now with our company at Hatfield.

I had managed to convince myself that there was no suitable engine available for the aeroplane, partly because it was probably true anyway and partly because I was very keen to design my own.

Years before, at Crux Easton, I had met a son of the

rector of the next village, and we became firm friends. His name was Gurth Churchill, and when his parents died and the family broke up Gurth came to London and became partner in an estate agency business with offices in Bedford Court Mansions. We shared digs in Shepherd's Bush and travelled by the Central London tube, Gurth to Tottenham Court Road and I to the City where I was working at that time in the drawing office of the Motor Omnibus Construction Company. Now I approached Gurth about letting me have a room in his offices. He kindly agreed, on very generous terms, and it was in this one-man drawing office that I started the drawings of the aeroplane engine. After setting out a number of types I finally decided to design a four-cylinder opposed or 'flat four' engine of about fifty horsepower, water-cooled and with ball bearings for main and big ends. The 'flat four' type of engine is now used in most American light planes, but differs in having a four-throw crankshaft in place of my two-throw, thus greatly improving balance.

The next items on the list were a workshop, and suitable tools and materials with which to equip it. Frank and I found a shed in Bothwell Street, Fulham, within reasonable distance of our flat which seemed to meet our needs, and it was only one pound per week rent. Today it seems unbelievable the amount that money would buy fifty years ago. All the tools we needed to build the aeroplane cost less than twenty pounds (consisting of planes, saws, chisels, files, gluepot, spoke-shave, vice, drill, etc.).

After finishing the drawings and tracings of the engine, I got a quotation for building it from the Iris Car Company of Willesden. Their price was two hundred and twenty pounds for the finished engine, and I tried not to show pleased surprise in accepting the figure. Later on the manager, whom I knew well, said they had not made much profit out of it. While the engine was being constructed I made various layouts of the aeroplane. With my limited knowledge of the aerodynamics side, I concentrated on the practical design of the structure, basing much on the few aeroplanes of that time that had made short flights. The main and dominating idea was to build something quickly and not too novel, because I felt the only way to learn was by experience, whether or not this ended in disaster. I decided to learn the hard way because, being dedicated to aeroplane design as well as to actual flying, it seemed essential to gain experience in everything, including learning to fly an aeroplane that had never flown, and might in fact be incapable of doing so. The final layout was a biplane with the engine mounted in the fuselage, with the crankshaft parallel with the wings and driving from each end of the shaft through bevel gears to two propellers turning in opposite directions. The Wright Brothers had used two propellers, but to get opposite rotation had used a crossed chain on one side. Bevel gears appealed to me as a better and sounder engineering job. Relatively few drawings were made of the aeroplane, and quite a bit of designing was done on the job.

It was at this time, May 1909, that I got married, with Gurth Churchill as best man. Louie Thomas had been governess to my sisters and younger brother, and companion-help to my mother at Crux Easton. We had been friends then, and later had fallen in love, becoming engaged soon after the aeroplane project began. Louie used to come to the shed to sew the wing fabric and make tea, but I think she had doubts about the outcome of our work and would have preferred something more down-to-earth. Almost all the materials we used could be bought at timber yards, ironmongers, steel tube makers or engineers' stores. The only 'special' items I can remember were turnbuckles for the bracing wires (ordinary piano wire), and the fabric which had a coating of cellulose dope on one side. During this time we increased our staff by engaging a boy as extra help.

One day Frank and I went, with some apprehension, to Willesden to see the first trial run of the engine. It ran quite well, and only minor modifications were necessary at this early stage. I was all for getting it into the airframe as soon as possible, and in fact it was installed before it had run a total of five hours. I was far too keen to start trying to fly to risk any longer engine test.

One day, A. V. Roe, whom I had met previously, came to see us and our aeroplane, and we talked for hours. Roe had got a 'hop' out of his triplane and asked us to visit him at Lea Marshes where he had a shed and tried out his machine. We went over and inspected his plane, but due to 'mechanical defects' which were even commoner then than they are today, we did not see it fly. It was fitted with a two-cylinder JAP motor cycle engine and the wing covering was strong wrapping paper, very light as compared with doped fabric. He progressed steadily, and today the name 'Avro' is world famous.

For some time I had been trying to find a suitable flying ground. Brooklands was too expensive and not, for me, sufficiently isolated, and the same applied to Eastchurch and Hendon. The final solution could not have been happier. When on a visit to Crux Easton I heard that Mr. Moore-Brabazon (now Lord Brabazon), had put up sheds at Seven Barrows, near Beacon Hill on Lord Carnarvon's estate, with the idea of taking a French biplane thére, but had later decided to use Eastchurch. In August 1909 Frank and I walked from Crux Easton over the downs to see the sheds and we agreed that they were very suitable, so I wrote to Moore-Brabazon and he agreed to sell. I bought the sheds for, I think, £150, the smaller one for a workshop and store, the larger for housing the aeroplane. These sheds were only three miles from Crux Easton and about five by road. In front of them was grass downland with ample space to fly an aeroplane of those days. It was a lovely and romantic place to go flying for the first time, and brought back many happy memories of Hampshire rambles and natural history expeditions as a boy. I walked carefully over the ground we should be using, heard larks singing high in the air, and was able to find two nests and mark their position with thin sticks so that we could avoid them when taxiing.

Looking back more than fifty years, I can see now that we must have been filled with a wonderful faith and optimism. Neither Frank nor I had even seen an aeroplane that could fly when we began work together. I had of course seen pictures of them in magazines, and was most influenced in the design of my own by the Wright Brothers' *Flyer* and the French Farmans, which in 1909 were already flying successfully. Before I actually flew successfully myself I did see one aircraft take off. In 1906 *The Daily Mail* had offered a prize of £10,000 for the first flight from London to Manchester. This was a daringly far-sighted offer, for at that time no one had flown in Europe, and four years passed before the prize was claimed. Claude Grahame-White's gallant pursuit of Louis Paulhan half-way across England in April 1910 has become too well-known an event in aeronautical history to describe again here, but I was at the Iris works examining progress on the engine when the word flashed round that Grahame-White was going to have a crack at the prize. He kept his Farman in the *Morning Post* shed at Wormwood Scrubs, and was going to take off on the wide stretch of common land there. We hurried over from Willesden, and were just in time to see his biplane box-kite rising hesitantly into the air and making off low over the roof-tops towards Manchester. This was a thrilling sight, but I could not claim that I had gained from it any practical hints on how to get an aircraft into the air.

In November, 1909, six months before Grahame-White's flight to Manchester, most of the work at the Fulham workshop was finished. The premises were not large enough to take our aeroplane fully erected, so we hired a lorry and drove it down in bits, together with the engine and tools.

One of the first things we had to get was some sort of motor transport, and I bought a much-used Panhard car from a friend for forty-five pounds. It had a four-cylinder engine and was called twelve horsepower. It was ancient and worn, but we kept it going with care and attention. About three miles from Seven Barrows in the village of Whitway there was a comfortable country inn in which Frank and I were able to stay. I usually went home to Louie in London for the week-ends, and sometimes to Crux Easton if we were not working. The inn was kept by a widow and her son. She was one of the kindest of women and looked after us for thirty shillings a week each, including the use of two bedrooms and a sitting-room. We took lunch with us to the sheds, and made tea there, returning to dinner in the evenings. In these pleasant conditions work on the aeroplane progressed. Fortunately we had very few visitors but one day Moore-Brabazon came with Lord Carnarvon, who was later associated with the discoveries of the tomb of Tutankhamen and who had kindly given me permission to use the ground and said he would see that the grass was kept mown. They examined our machine with interest and were encouraging, but I doubt whether they seriously considered it would ever fly. The local people, on the other hand, were confident that we would be taking off within days of our arrival. But after a month of silence and no sign of the machine sailing overhead, they lost all interest in us, except I suppose as that pair of cranks up on the downs.

Aeroplane controls at this time had not been standardized. The movements controlling the elevators and ailerons were obvious and instinctive, but the rudder bar raised the question, should it be treated as the handlebars of a bicycle, pushing the right-hand end to turn left and vice versa? This way seemed natural to me and so it was connected. Later on I found the opposite way was standard, and I had the diffiult job of 'unlearning' my way and learning the new, standard way. It took quite some time.

*

One day in December 1909 we opened the doors of our shed wide and pushed our assembled aeroplane out on to the field for the first time for an engine run. The propellers and gearing had not yet turned over under power, and it was a great moment when we started up the four-cylinder motor and watched the twin propellers rotating behind the two wings like great paddles, catching the winter sun on their blades. I opened the throttle wider, and the rising roar of the engine rolled over the downland, scattering the birds, while Frank stood close. After a few minutes I cut the ignition and when the propellers had stopped rotating, I climbed down and we looked them over carefully. The propellers each had two aluminium blades attached to a single steel tube passing through the steel hub, and the pitch could be set by altering the angle and twist of the blade by means of clips and clamping screws. Miraculously, everything seemed to be all right.

'I'll give her another run,' I said and climbed back into the seat, while Frank stood by ready to swing the pro-pellers. The engine started easily again and for a time everything seemed to be going well—almost unbelievably well for a first trial. Then, with a sudden screeching sound, a bevel gearbox collapsed and I cut off at once.

Over the next weeks, when I carried out the first taxiing trials, we endured a whole series of failures and disap-pointments, the almost certain lot of anyone pioneering in a field as new as heavier-than-air travel. We expected them, and were not too downcast, but our patience was often sorely tested. No sooner had we replaced the light aluminium gearbox casing, which had collapsed so readily, with heavier aluminium bronze ones, than we began to suffer transmission trouble. Our propellers were set symmetrically, but one day when we cut the engine we could see when they stopped rotating that the blades of one were horizontal while those of the other were vertical. This could only mean a failure in the shafts or gearing, and when we made an examination we found that one of the driving shafts had twisted, only slightly, but enough to cause a disaster if I had been in the air. I had foolishly, though partly for economy, used ordinary commercial quality steel tubes for these shafts, with the end fittings pegged and brazed in. The simplest and quickest cure was to fit heavier gauge steel tubes, but I was already having doubts about the whole propeller arrangement, which I suspected was heavy as well as clumsy. Our next trouble was with the carburetter, which I had designed and built myself. So we fitted a standard Claudel instead.

And so we progressed, day after day and often far into the night, in our £50 workshop, working away, refining, adjusting, experimenting and, we hoped, improving. From time to time we opened the shed doors and took the machine out for more taxiing trials.

Our machine obstinately refused to get off the ground. This apparently fatal blow to our hopes fell on us slowly, as day after day passed and, no matter what speed I persuaded out of the 'plane, she showed not the slightest tendency to lift. On many mornings conditions were unsuitable in any case, for the wind would be blowing too strongly, or from the wrong direction. What we needed was a very gentle steady breeze blowing up the slight incline of the field, and we found no better way of judging this than by the well-tried handkerchief method. Many times we would motor out to the field when the weather seemed promising, shake out a handkerchief, only to find it blowing in the wrong direction, or billowing out at too acute an angle.

I think it was a mixture of impatience and sheer will power that finally got the first de Havilland machine off on its first flight. And it was crass ignorance that caused it to come back again, violently and disastrously. The sudden stress was too much for the wings, which probably had a pretty fine margin of strength anyway. But as I picked myself dizzily out of the wreckage to be received by anxious inquiries from Frank and Hereward—and a few minutes later from my severely shaken father—I could see that it was not only the wings that had gone. There was little but the engine left to salvage. The fuselage was splintered into small pieces and one propeller with its gearing was battered and bent, although the other had survived, out of sheer spite I feel, to give me a last vicious blow.

We did not waste any time on regrets or prolonged farewells. We said good-bye to our kindly landlady but gave not a backward glance to the field and sheds. We would be back again soon enough. A lorry was already on the way to collect the remnants of our first machine. At Fulham we could begin work at once. We felt no real sense of disappointment, for all the time we had been at Seven Barrows I think we had both thought subconsciously that our first trials would probably end in disaster. But this time, we knew, we would build an aeroplane that would fly.

CHAPTER FOUR

AIRBORNE

Bᴀᴄᴋ at Fulham, Frank and I took stock of our remnants and resources and made our plans for the second machine. Money was already running low, and speed and simplicity of materials and construction were essential. On the other hand, it had clearly been a mistake to economize on the propellers, shafts and gearing. We therefore did away with the troublesome twin propellers, turned the engine at right angles and mounted a single wooden propeller direct on the engine shaft, which meant we could dispose of the heavy flywheel. We also lightened and simplified the landing gear, using now two bicycle-type wheels and a rear skid, and constructed a lighter, simpler and more robust main structure. By the summer of 1910 we were ready again. We hired the same lorry, took Number Two down to Hampshire, and put her in the big shed bordering the field at Seven Barrows.

This time everything went much better. It required only two or three weeks of taxiing trials and minor adjustments before I felt confident enough to attempt to become airborne. The engine was working well, I felt that I had got the 'hang' of the controls and that real flight was at last possible. All the same, I determined to be less impulsive than before.

It was a beautiful evening in late summer, and I had already run the machine several times fast into the light breeze, feeling my way along with the light touches on the rudder bar and gentle pressure backwards on the control stick. I pulled up alongside Frank, who had been watching the machine's behaviour keenly from the centre of the field.

'I'm going to try one more run,' I called to him above the sound of the engine. 'I'm not sure, but I think I'm almost leaving the ground. Anyway, I'm not feeling any bumps. Will you lie down as I go past and watch if you can see any daylight between the wheels and the grass?'

Frank agreed, and I took the machine back up the slight slope again, turned and took a line that would pass close beside his prostrate body. I opened the throttle and accelerated towards him. I was going faster than ever before as I approached, and eased back a little more of the stick, keeping her on a straight course with the rudder bar. I must have been travelling at 25 or 30 m.p.h. when I passed beside him, and at once eased back, coming to a halt at the bottom of the field.

A few seconds later Frank ran up alongside me. He was shouting and gesticulating and I cut off the ignition in order to hear what he was saying. 'You flew all right,' he told me excitedly. 'You were several inches off the ground for about twenty yards. Well done.'

I climbed out of the seat, exhilarated at my achievement and scarcely able to believe that I had actually flown—in a 'plane that we had built ourselves. Those three or four inches meant more to me than the thousands of feet which separated me from the ground later when I took the altitude record. I believe this was the most important and memorable moment of my life. There was some justification for my excitement, for if I was able to take the machine up to six inches and come back safely to earth, there was no reason why I should not with equal ease rise to six hundred feet, so long as I took things slowly and carefully. But it was most important that I should keep my enthusiasm and eagerness under control. Not only was I flying for the first time, teaching myself as I went along, but I was flying a prototype experimental machine which I had built largely out of my head and with no previous experience. From our point of view this was double pioneering work, and if we failed again, if I crashed and wrecked Number Two, I knew it would be the end of flying and of the career I had planned.

'That's enough for one day, I think,' I said to Frank, who agreed when I suggested we should go back to the inn and discuss very carefully, step by step, how we should develop our flying programme. I also decided, now that we had proved that our machine could get me into the air, that Louie should come down from Kensington to join us and see us through the trials. She had, after all, helped to build both machines, working for hundreds of hours on her sewing machine stitching the stiff doped wing fabric, and was really a part of the company. She still had reservations about the whole project, especially after the first crash, and even when I wrote that night, telling her that I had flown, I think she was more alarmed than excited. She left London two days later, and I met her in the Panhard at Newbury Station. I was glad to have her with me during the exciting but anxious weeks that lay ahead, especially as she was expecting our first child. A few weeks later our son, Geoffrey, was born at Crux Easton, arriving in this world as I was beginning to fly farther and higher than ever before.

At first our progress was very slow. From that first flight, I took the machine a few more inches and then feet off the ground, but on many days there was too much wind or it was from the wrong direction, or, maddeningly, if the weather was suitable, we were busy repairing a wing-tip or the undercarriage from a previous misadventure. I had known from the beginning that the most difficult thing of all that I should have to learn was landing. I understood the theory well enough, that the aeroplane had to lose flying speed and begin to stall at the most only a foot or two above the ground. If she was stalled too high, we would go straight in, as we had on that first occasion. I had been lucky then and could not expect Providence to be so kind again. On the other hand, if I made contact with the ground while the speed was above the point of stall, I should take off again, probably bouncing along in kangaroo-like leaps, damaging the propeller and landing gear. I had no way of judging my speed over the ground except by the pressure of air against my face, the sound of the wind passing over the wings, and the noise level of the engine and propeller. All this I had to learn by trial and error, taking off on longer and longer hops, until another momentous day, many weeks after that first brief skim over the grass, when I made the sudden decision to continue while I was airborne, easing the machine very carefully higher and higher, until I was beyond the point when I could land again in a straight line. I rose up above the road bordering our field, up to some fifty feet, then gently banked and turned to the left in a half circle. I levelled out and continued downwind, moving the controls gently in turn to left and to right and up and down, banked to the left again and straightened up when I had completed the full 360 degrees. The field lay ahead of me and at an appalling distance below; and it was manifestly inevitable that somehow or other I should have to get back on to it again.

I reduced throttle and tipped the nose slightly forward, aiming the machine towards the point where I had begun the taxiing run. I could see Frank standing close to the sheds, his face pointed up towards me, looking very small. Then I gave all my mind to the task of losing height and placing the 'plane, slowly and gently, back where it had come from. I progressively reduced the propeller revolutions and held back on the stick until I calculated that I had achieved the correct angle and speed of glide just above stalling point and watched the dull blur of green ahead come nearer. While I was still at about ten feet I eased the throttle right back and began the last levelling out. The machine settled, struck the ground once rather hard, rose momentarily and came back to earth on its wheels and skid. In a few yards we were at rest, and seconds later Frank was at my side.

From this flight confidence grew at a great pace. The 'plane did not have the endurance for more than local hops and circuits, but as I took her up day after day without mishap, sometimes to as high as a hundred feet, I felt ready to attempt more elaborate manœuvres. Figures of eight became a commonplace and I made some steep banked turns without mishap. One day I said to Frank, 'I think it's time you had a flight. How do you feel?' He had obviously longed to be asked and accepted the suggestion excitedly. We fixed a passenger seat to the main frame behind the pilot's, Frank climbed in and we went right up to a hundred feet without difficulty. A few days later I suggested to Louie that she might have a ride. However nervous she may have felt about our future while I continued to indulge my passion for flying and for aeroplanes, she had recognized by then that there was no deterring me and that therefore she should give me all possible encouragement. I think she agreed because she knew it would please me and that she felt it her duty to show her interest in our work. So she came over from Crux Easton one afternoon in the pony and trap with young Geoffrey in her arms, and climbed gamely into the second seat. I think she enjoyed her flight, too, and at eight weeks of age, Geoffrey must, at that time, have been the youngest person in the world to go up.

By November 1910, I could begin to consider myself quite a proficient pilot, and I knew that, in spite of its faults, our second aeroplane could be counted a success. A year or two later, of course, almost nobody taught themselves to fly as people like Blériot, the Wright Brothers,

Cody, Roe, I and a few others had done. Instead you learnt to fly with an instructor. Most of the professional flying instruction one received even in the very early days was admirable, but I don't think it is bigoted to say that self-taught flying produced the better and safer pilot. Some did not survive, of course, but those who did, because everything was self-taught and learnt at first hand, never forgot. The orthodox method of instruction, then as now, was to go up with an instructor and gradually take an increasingly greater share of the responsibility for the 'plane until thought to be proficient enough to 'go solo'. Another more drastic method, tried during the First World War, was on the survival-of-the-fittest principle. It was known as the Gosport School and was inaugurated by that gifted pilot, Major R. R. Smith-Barry. After only a few hops, the pupil was taken up and treated to a rapid series of evolutions, from loops to rolls and spins. On return to earth, if the pupil staggered away groaning, he was considered unworthy of further instruction; if he was sane and obviously in his right mind, the training programme continued.

'Instructed' pilots did, however, experience a pleasure which we few self-taught pilots rarely enjoyed. The spectacle and excitement of being above the earth and viewing it from a new perspective and without distraction, in those early days must have been very wonderful. But I cannot recall experiencing in my earliest flying any new or exceptional emotions, or of responding to the simple fact of being airborne, because it occurred through progressively longer hops over an extended period of time, and because all my attention was keyed to the necessity of operating the controls correctly, by trial and error; in short, of maintaining our machine, and myself, in one piece, in the air.

Only one other occasion after that first successful flight stands out as an exciting emotional experience from all my

E

flying before the 1914 War, and that was my first attempt
to probe into the clouds. Very few people attempted to do
this before the days of instruments, for it was inevitably
accompanied by some degree of risk. But the attainment of
sheer height was something I always strived for, and one
overcast day after I had left Seven Barrows, and in a later
'plane, I climbed at maximum speed and allowed myself
to be swallowed by the low cloud, attempting to maintain
only by instinct and a sense of balance the same angle and
attitude as before. Some tense minutes passed, and then as
I broke clear of the damp darkness that had enveloped me
during my ascent, I suddenly found myself in a blinding
world of billowing whiteness that stretched in every direction, magnificent and vast and thrilling. Besides the
wonderful peace and beauty of the scene, there was also a
complete absence of the motion and turbulence that always
accompanied flying, particularly in small light aircraft,
beneath or in cloud. This was a flying experience I can
never forget.

By the late autumn of 1910 Frank Hearle and I had to
face the curious situation of being in possession of a flying
machine of our own design which worked as well as most
others and better than some, but which appeared to have
no immediate commercial future. Certainly I had no
means of promoting Number Two and marketing it to the
very few people who were prepared to buy an aeroplane at
that time. Frank and I had no regular jobs to turn to, and
my grandfather's thousand pounds was just about
exhausted.

We were in the throes of this dilemma when a most
fortunate and for me momentous meeting took place. It
is extraordinary how perhaps once in a lifetime the right
person is met at the right time, with far-reaching conse-
quences. For me the person was Fred Green, the occasion
the Olympia Show in 1910, just when Frank and I were
almost on the point of giving up. Fred Green had been

a friend of mine ever since I had known him when he had been on the engineering side of Daimlers at Coventry. He caught sight of me in one of the aisles at Olympia, and approached me at once in his abrupt manner, smiling and calling out in his high-pitched voice, 'Hullo, Geoffrey, what are you doing now? Still on motor buses?'

'I've finished with buses, I hope for ever,' I told him. 'I've made an engine, and an aeroplane that flies all right, but now I've got to sell it or get a job—preferably both. What are you doing?'

By an odd coincidence, Green had also got into the very small field of aeronautics, although on a rather different level. 'I'm engineer at the Factory at Farnborough, but we only deal with dirigible balloons.'

In the foetid atmosphere of Olympia, and amid the sounds of a hundred thousand other voices, we talked for a while about flying and what we had been doing. Then Green said, quite casually, 'A fellow called Mervyn O'Gorman is Superintendent at Farnborough, and he and I are keen to have aeroplanes as well as balloons. Why not offer him yours, and ask for a job at the same time?'

This seemed an opportunity to do something with our machine that couldn't be missed. I said good-bye to him and promised that I would write off to O'Gorman. I received a prompt reply and went off almost at once for an appointment with him at his home in Embankment Gardens, Chelsea. I was armed with a roll of drawings and a quite atrocious photograph of my aeroplane, and with these I was presumptive enough to believe that I might sell to the War Office their first military machine. In fact, I was not very hopeful, and had to confess to myself that the one and only piece of real evidence on which I could base my salesmanship was the photograph, which did at least show Number Two in the air.

I was reassured at once when O'Gorman greeted me. He was a tall, slim man, balding and with a round clean-shaven face that expressed kindness and humour as well as intelligence. I was soon to discover that he possessed wide scientific knowledge and mechanical and electrical engineering experience. 'Green has told me about your aeroplane,' he told me at once. 'Let's have a look at those drawings.'

I unrolled them and explained somewhat apologetically that although those for the engine were complete, the 'plane itself had been made mostly from rough sketches. 'I'm afraid I don't know much about aeroplanes anyway, and almost no theory at all,' I said lamely.

'I shouldn't worry about that,' O'Gorman replied cheerfully. 'Very few people know anything really reliable about them. It's still mostly a matter of trial and error. At Farnborough we're very keen to start on aeroplanes, but the snag is that the War Office people haven't got much faith in them and it's not going to be easy to persuade them. They want to put everything into airships. So if we're going to make a start with yours, keep your price as low as possible and I'll try to persuade them to agree to buy.'

O'Gorman looked through the drawings again and asked me how much I thought I would want. I was unprepared for this question and had absolutely no idea what to suggest. However, I had to say something. 'What about four hundred pounds? Does that sound sensible?'

O'Gorman agreed that it did. 'But you will have to do some sort of acceptance trial, probably an hour's flight without making any serious adjustments to your machine.'

That left only one important point unsettled. I certainly could not consider leaving Frank Hearle out of this and suggested that he should come along with me if my aeroplane was bought. 'I'll need somebody else with experience of aeroplanes,' I said, 'especially if kites and balloons are the only things anyone knows anything about at Farnborough.' O'Gorman readily agreed to this, and I left him with my grateful thanks, to endure the inevitable period of waiting before I should hear whether or not the War Office would change its mind about aeroplanes.

It was an anxious time for us. The days spun out into weeks, and still there was no word about our aeroplane. Frank and I filled in the time by doing some more flying down at Seven Barrows, but pleasant though this was, it did not advance our plans at all. We had learned all we could from the machine and we could not afford to make any more modifications or experiments. In fact money was becoming seriously short, and I knew we could not hold out much longer.

Then at last, just before Christmas 1910, a letter arrived from O'Gorman. Frank was beside me at the time, and he watched me in silence as I opened it. 'I'm sure they've turned it down,' I said in despair.

I was wrong. By agreeing to buy the machine for the suggested figure of £400 and to taking me on to supervise its development and to design new machines, with Frank as mechanic, Fred Green and O'Gorman had truly launched me off on my long career in the aircraft business. And Jason Saunders's faith had been fulfilled at last. On his thousand pounds I had designed and built two aeroplanes, complete with engine, one of which had flown successfully, paid a staff of two, and kept myself and family, with a car, for some eighteen months. With this £400 I now had a substantial credit in the bank, and wrote to my grandfather offering to repay part of my debt. 'You keep it, my boy,' he replied, 'You'll need it later.' I was obliged to tell myself that he was probably right.

CHAPTER FIVE

FARNBOROUGH DAYS

A WHITEHALL memorandum dated April 1909 makes interesting reading today, and reflects clearly the vacillation and uncertainty of official policy towards flying at that time. 'The War Office has decided,' it ran, 'to cease making experiments with aeroplanes as the cost has proved to be too great, namely £2,500.' And yet, a little more than eighteen months later they were prepared to buy my aeroplane and employ Frank and me on research work at Farnborough. In 1906 J. W. Dunne (later the author of that curious and puzzling work *An Experiment in Time*) had been attached to the Factory at Farnborough in order to carry out full scale tests on an inherently stable aeroplane of his own design. Ever since 1903 Dunne had been working closely with model gliders, and had advanced considerably to a machine based on the vee shape of a zanonia seed, which he had observed was a good glider. The first trials were carried out in secret at Blair Atholl in Perthshire in Scotland in 1907, where a successful short glide was made. But the machine crashed soon after. In July 1908 a new machine, the Dunne III, was taken to Blair Atholl and made a few power glides, but the French R.E.P. engine powering it was quite unreliable. Shortly after this the experimental work petered out, although Dunne later, and working on his own, produced both a biplane and a monoplane that were stable and flew well, but were slow and were never given the development they deserved.

The main work at Farnborough, the development of man-carrying kites, balloons, semi-rigid and non-rigid airships, continued while Dunne was at work on his own with a small specialized staff. There was a good deal of inter-departmental jealousy between these various branches, and the atmosphere was not at this time a very congenial one. I have no doubt that the combined hostility of the kite and lighter-than-air branches had killed Dunne's work almost before he had begun, and I was conscious of this suspicious regard for the upstart aeroplane on the day of my arrival when some of the balloon men merely watched our strenuous efforts to unload and erect our aeroplane in dour silence and made no move to assist us. The airship people at least had some cause for anxiety about the imminent obsolescence of their craft, and their own future at the Factory. Sometimes it seemed as if nothing could go right for them. They had bought a French Lebaudy airship, which was housed in the largest of the airships sheds. One day when it was being brought out for a trial flight the top of the gas bag was pierced and ripped by some projection from the roof and collapsed. After extensive repairs and alterations to the shed, the Lebaudy eventually appeared safely from it and rose to a hundred feet or so—when the gas bag suddenly kinked in the middle the whole took on a vee shape, and sank gracefully to the ground. Later it was persuaded to make some brief circuits of Farnborough in calm weather. Unfortunately there was a slight rise in wind speed, the airship got quite out of control, was blown over the edge of the Common and draped itself over a private house on the main road. No one was seriously hurt, but that was the end of the Lebaudy. Beta, Gamma and Delta were the three locally designed and built airships. The first two did a certain amount of somewhat tentative flying, but the much bigger Delta, intended originally as a semi-rigid machine with a girder framework lying on each side of the gas bag and with control cabin and engines suspended below was not a success and had to be abandoned in this form. It was the last airship to be constructed at Farnborough.

There were even more powerful forces at work outside the Factory to prevent design and construction of aircraft, and these were represented by the new aircraft manufacturers and their own trade organizations and journals. They succeeded ultimately in preventing us officially from designing new aircraft. But there was nothing to stop us repairing or reconstructing damaged ones, and we quietly got round this ruling by making use of odd pieces of crashed machines and 'reconstructing' them—adding our own ideas here and there—into entirely new 'planes. A victory by this group that was quite as serious as the adoption of this regulation was the final dismissal, after a long battle, of O'Gorman. Mervyn O'Gorman was a farsighted and brilliant administrator who did great work for British aeronautics during his brief reign as superintendent at Farnborough. He was utterly convinced of the superiority of the aeroplane over all forms of lighter-than-air craft, revealing this persuasion early on in his administration in April 1911 by changing the name from the Army Balloon Factory to the Army Aircraft Factory, and twelve months later to the Royal Aircraft Factory. O'Gorman was no yes-man, and there were certain officials at the War Office who believed that scientists should always yield to their demands. He was also persistently hounded down by two men, one the editor of an aeronautical 'trade' journal, and the other an unreliable and eccentric person, Pemberton Billing, who was connected with the trade and later became an M.P., concluding his career in the lower House by being carried out kicking and screaming. It was Billing and this editor who forced O'Gorman to give up designing and building aircraft at Farnborough, resorting to gross exaggeration to back up their case and flinging so much mud at O'Gorman in the process that some senior officers at the War Office, in their craven weakness, gave him to understand that he was no longer needed. A disastrous result of this victory was the immediate cessation of much interesting research which—to quote only one example— might well have led to the earlier development of variable pitch propellers. O'Gorman was a most powerful and likeable character with wide interests and hobbies that varied from painting to lacquer work, in all of which he excelled right up to his death in 1958 at the age of eighty-eight. I lost touch with 'O'G', as he was always called, for some years after his departure from Farnborough, but we re-established our friendship when we were both old men and I frequently visited him in the same house in Chelsea in which he had interviewed me—and ushered me into the wide world of aeronautics.

However, when Frank and I arrived at Farnborough from Seven Barrows with our aeroplane, O'Gorman was in full power and had recently succeeded in reversing the War Office's decision to cease all work on heavier-than-air machines. We still had to prove our aeroplane's airworthiness and acquire the Royal Aero Club's certificate by flying for one hour. I carried out this test in January 1911, in bitterly cold weather which forced me to make two landings after twenty and forty minutes in order to thaw out. Winter flying at that time, in cockpits as exposed to the elements as a motor cycle—but without the comforting warmth of an engine between your knees—was for the robust only. My aeroplane was duly awarded the certificate and became known as F.E.1. I had no idea what this meant at first, for the naming of aircraft at Farnborough origi-nated in the most obscure and illogical formula that even the Civil Service could devise. For some unknown reason, all early aircraft nomenclature was based on French air-craft types, and I later discovered that F.E.1 meant 'Farman Experimental Number One' because, like the

73

Farman, my aeroplane had a pusher propeller. B.E. stood for 'Blériot Experimental' because the Blériot had a tractor propeller, while all machines that were 'tail-first' or canard 'planes were known as S.E., or 'Santos Dumont Experimental'; although later, just to confuse things further, S.E. stood for 'Scout Experimental'. Very few people, even at Farnborough, understood the system.

As soon as F.E.1 had passed its test, Louie and I with the baby moved into rooms at Farnborough for a short time before renting a small house not far from the Factory. It was in this house that our second son, Peter, was born in 1913. Louie was delighted at my new status and the sense of security we now enjoyed, and during the early period there, before the restrictions on our activities were imposed, I found the work more exciting and fulfilling than anything I had done before. As the only test pilot, I was able to combine flying with designing, and take advantage of the help of those on the technical staff who specialized in stressing and aerodynamics. The facilities for construction and static testing too, were of a standard we had never even contemplated when Frank and I had been working in our shed at Fulham and at Seven Barrows.

The first design I did at Farnborough in 1910–11 was an improvement in many details of Number Two, or F.E.1. The new machine was powered by a fifty-horsepower Gnome rotary engine and had a crude fabric-covered cockpit and small windscreen which provided some welcome protection for the pilot. I did a lot of flying on this new machine, the F.E.2, including tests for the Royal Aero Club's Special Certificate which involved a cross country flight of one hundred miles there and back and landing on a given mark from two thousand feet without using the engine. My certificate was No. 4.

F.E.2 distinguished itself in another way. The landing gear was removed, F.E.2 was then mounted on a single plywood float and I was able to fly it off Fleet Pond, about three miles from the Factory. In 1911 this was still considered a daring innovation, although I was certainly not the first to try it. The small islands and the swans had to be avoided and made take-off and landing a trifle hazardous.

The canard type seemed to promise some advantages and we made one by 'reconstructing' a Blériot fitted with an E.N.V. engine. This Blériot was damaged at Salisbury Plain and was known as the 'Man Killer'. The only vestige of the 'Man Killer' in the new canard, S.E.1, was the engine. At first we fitted rudders at the rear on outriggers, but nearer to the main planes than usual. Turning with these rudders was not very satisfactory so they were discarded and a single rudder was mounted on the nose of the long fuselage which extended forward and on which was also mounted the front plane and elevators. This rudder worked well in the air but, having no slipstream over it, was useless for ground steering. Under these conditions take-off was tricky and uncertain because until one reached flying speed there was no steering control and a slight side wind could turn the 'plane off course possibly towards an obstruction, such as high trees. I intended to overcome this trouble by fitting a steering nose wheel (as used in most aircraft today), but it was not to be. An official at the Factory who had only got his 'ticket' a week before said he wanted to fly S.E.1. I told him he couldn't because the rudder control still required modification and was too dangerous for a beginner. It had no effect. He was a religious fanatic and believed Providence looked after his every action. He had only been in the air for five minutes when he stalled and spun into the ground, dying within minutes. So the tradition of 'Man Killer' was sustained.

In 1911 there was a definite trend in design in favour of the tractor type as against the pusher type. Being in full agreement with this trend, I lost interest in the canard which, in any case, was smashed beyond repair, and concentrated on the design of a tractor biplane, B.E.1.

The B.E.1 (the B.E.2 was similar except for the engine) was my most ambitious and most successful design up to April 1911. I discussed the design with Fred Green and had limited help from the primitive stressing and aerodynamics of those days. Because the ban on new design and construction was then in force, B.E.1 was 'reconstructed' from the wreckage of a Voisin plane, presented, in pieces, to the Government by the Duke of Westminster. Actually the only unit used from the wreckage was the Wolseley engine, a sixty-horsepower, water-cooled eight-cylinder vee type, which had luckily escaped damage. Long exhaust pipes were fitted which acted to some extent as silencers, and the Press exaggerated this feature and referred to the machine as 'The New Silent Army Aeroplane'.

I looked after the actual design of B.E.1 and made most of the detail drawings with a junior draughtsman named Folland to help me. Folland later became a brilliant designer and formed Folland Aircraft Limited, producing the jet fighter, the Gnat, before retiring from industry to become a recluse. The B.E.1 and B.E.2 were orthodox biplanes, chiefly of wood construction, with welded steel tube for tailplane, elevators and rudder. For lateral control I reverted to 'wing warping' as used by the Wright Brothers and also by Blériot. The wings 'warped' about the fixed front spar by moving the rear spar up or down. The position of the front spar in the wing was important, and I had to make a guess, and my guess was a bit out. This resulted in the wing 'taking charge' in gusty weather so that the wings tended to 'warp' the pilot instead of the pilot warping the wings. The trouble was largely overcome by fitting restraining springs. On future aircraft we reverted to orthodox ailerons which were more satisfactory. But B.E.2s had a long and successful career. Fitted

76

with the seventy-horsepower eight-cylinder air-cooled Renault engine, the top speed was seventy-two miles per hour with a very low landing speed. On one of the early B.E.2s I was able to gain the British height record with Major Sykes, Commandant of the Royal Flying Corps, as passenger. This was in August 1912 during the Military Aircraft Trials on Salisbury Plain. We reached 10,500 feet, having passed through two layers of cloud. We were perished with cold, and as the aeroplane also seemed to suffer and would go no higher we came down to 1,000 feet, and having no idea where we were, I picked up a railway line, followed it to a station, and came down low enough to read the name which turned out to be Hermitage, just north of Newbury, my old home town. It was easy to fly from here back to Salisbury Plain. We had been in the air for about three and a half hours. This height record stood for about three years.

I liked Major Sykes, and we became good friends. He was not at all like the typical soldier or airman in manner or appearance, but far more like a scholar or university don. Of slim build, with a soft voice and great charm of manner, he was an almost exact opposite of his successor, the great 'Boom' Trenchard, who was really responsible for the founding of a separate Air Force in 1918. Sykes later became Sir Frederick Sykes, and held several important posts, including that of Governor of Bombay. I felt deeply touched when I heard from Lady Sykes after his death in 1954 that he had expressed a wish that I should scatter his ashes from the air over Salisbury Plain where he lived, and where we had taken off for our memorable flight more than forty years before. And this I did.

There were several people at Farnborough in 1914 who became distinguished figures in science and industry in later years, and others who died early in the cause of aviation. Among the former was the dour and rather forbidding Frederick Alexander Lindemann, later Lord

Cherwell, who worked in the Physics Department. I never really came to know him until he came to lunch at Hatfield during the Second World War. George Thomson and William Farren were others, both of whom were knighted. Among the pilots who joined me on the testing side were Ronald Kemp, Winfield Smith and Norman Spratt.

But 'Colonel' Cody was surely the most colourful and picturesque of the Farnborough characters. S. F. Cody— a friend but no relation of Buffalo Bill Cody—had actually left the Factory before my arrival, but I had known him three years earlier in 1907 when he had tried out a radiator I had patented in his airship *Nulli Secundus*, which had previously suffered from overheating, and incidentally continued to do so after my modification. In spite of this trouble, Cody and his friend Colonel Capper succeeded in flying the airship on a record flight in October 1907 from Farnborough to London at an average speed of 16 m.p.h., although they had to land at the Crystal Palace on the return journey because of a head wind. While at the Factory Cody had been engaged on experimental work with man-lifting kites, dirigible balloons and aeroplanes. Cody was, and looked, something of an adventurer, and was a pure individualist and a lovable character. He must have weighed all of fifteen stone, and his naturally dramatic appearance was emphasized by his small goatee beard, waxed moustache and long hair which fell over his shoulders when it was not tucked in under the cowboy hat which he usually wore. Cody had been born in Texas and had led a cowpuncher's life for some years, becoming a highly skilled horseman and an expert in lassoing and other tricks. He was also an expert with gun and rifle and had shot numerous buffaloes, or bison, for supplying meat to camps of railway workers. He had spent two years panning for gold in the Klondike rush, but in spite of this and his cowboy background he neither smoked, drank nor swore.

78

Having known horses all his life, he could stand up to the best horse-dealers anywhere and he did a lot of honest (as far as it can be) horse dealing in England when he first came here. He also promoted races and gave shows of his exceptional horsemanship. He met the daughter of one of his horseman acquaintances, fell in love and married her, which incidentally enabled him to satisfy one of his early ambitions and put on stage plays of his own. Mrs. Cody was the golden-haired heroine, Cody the villain, and as his sons Leon and Vivian grew up they were added to the cast. These plays were good old melodramatic stuff with plenty of lurid events. The 'company' toured England, playing at the smaller towns in any sort of building or barn available. But his restlessness led him back to another of his early ambitions—kite-flying. Ever since he had flown his first kite in America when very young, he had had thoughts of building much larger kites that might lift a man. The experiments went well and resulted in his actually interesting the War Office in them, eventually demonstrating their capabilities at the Balloon Factory at Farnborough.

Cody's method was to send up three or four kites, equally spaced on a single steel cable. A much larger kite was then sent up the cable and from this kite a deep basket was suspended on a short cable. In this basket crouched a very brave man. The transition from these kites to much larger and more complex aeroplanes was inevitable, and Cody started to design and construct his first aeroplane in 1907. In May 1908 he began official trials on Laffan's Plain, using the fifty-horsepower Antoinette engine that had been used in *Nulli Secundus*. In October 1908 he made a straight flight of over four hundred yards, but in April 1909 all this came to an end with the War Office edict to cease experiments with aeroplanes. Cody then set up on his own on Laffan's Plain. I used often to fly over there to talk flying to this fascinating and brilliant character. His enthusiasm and practical, down-to-earth approach were infectious. He had built his own aeroplane himself with almost no theoretical knowledge nor mathematics, and judged the strength of things and the fitness of detail parts purely by eye. He used bamboo extensively in his biplane and fixed the steel bracing wires by tying them in knots at the end fittings with his enormously strong hands. In spite of his makeshift methods, many of his aeroplanes flew successfully and won competitions.

Early one morning, while still in bed, I heard the unmistakable note of Cody's open exhaust as he flew round Laffan's Plain. Suddenly the sound was cut off, as cleanly as if by a switch, and never restarted. Later I heard with great sorrow that this silence had signalled the end of his last flight. It had been a catastrophic break-up in mid-air, and both Cody and his passenger were killed instantly.[1]

Edward Busk was another great figure at Farnborough in those early days. He joined the Factory in 1912 from Cambridge and started research work on stability and control. Busk was brilliantly clever, and not entirely in his chosen sphere. He combined theory with sound practice and soon converted a B.E.2—an unstable aeroplane—into a B.E.2C, which had a high degree of stability and could be flown 'hands and feet off'. Busk was very likeable and entirely without 'side'. Round-faced and smiling, he was anything but the typical brainy scientist. He often came round to our house in the evenings and sang songs in a boyish voice and rather out of tune. He was very keen on rock climbing, and his eye would rove round our sitting-room in search of something that might offer scope for a demonstration, but my wife was never very encouraging. Not long after he had converted the B.E.2C we were flying together over Laffan's Plain at dusk in November 1914 in different machines. His B.E.2C was some distance beneath

[1] For a full account of Cody's life see *Pioneer of the Air* by G. A. Broomfield.

me, dimly silhouetted against the dark ground, looking perfectly normal and flying apparently satisfactorily. Suddenly and without any warning, flames shot out of his engine, in seconds reaching to beyond the tail. The B.E.2C's nose tipped forward, evidently beyond all control, and then went straight towards the ground like a flaming torch. Poor Busk must have been dead before the crash, but after circling the flaming wreck I flew back to the Factory and ferried several men over to see if they could do anything. It was a tragic loss for his family and for aviation. The sight of Busk's flaming aeroplane going down was very terrible, and for long afterwards I would wake up in the middle of the night from dreams in which I saw it all happen again.

Dr. Keith Lucas, another great scientist at Farnborough who did much valuable research and work on compasses, also crashed fatally at about the same time, in a collision over Salisbury Plain. A tremendous amount of trouble-free flying went on, of course, even at that time, but as in all pioneering work, the risks were inevitably quite high. After all, we knew very little about what we were doing, and had no certain knowledge, for example, even on which was the safer, the biplane or the monoplane. Blériot had favoured the monoplane for his cross-Channel machine, but in 1912 the biplane was definitely in favour, and there were only two Army monoplanes on manoeuvres in that year. Monoplanes, with their reduced resistance, were accepted as being faster, but speed at that time, when to get off the ground, fly safely and return were enough, was of no importance. Take-off and landing were the most difficult and dangerous operations, and the biplane with its larger wing area and therefore lower loading allowed lower landing and take-off speeds. The wing-loading of biplanes in 1909 and 1910 was about 3 lb. for each square foot of wing area. With the coming of the monoplane as the demand rose for greater speed for both commercial and military purposes, the wing-loading and landing speed rose higher and higher, until on modern jet machines loadings of 80 lb. are not uncommon. The use of slots and flaps reduces the landing speed somewhat, but it is usually around 80 or 90 m.p.h., compared with the 28 or 30 m.p.h. of the F.E.1. The early biplanes were also more reliable structurally than monoplanes. This was shown tragically in the Army Manœuvres of 1912 when both monoplanes crashed, killing all their crews. I was flying a B.E.2 at the time and landed to inspect the wreckage of one of them. It was spread over a large area, indicating a progressive break-up in the air. There was no question of collision as the two accidents were far separated in time and distance.

'Flutter', which was scarcely understood in 1912 was the probable cause. The rigidly braced structure of the biplane made it far less prone to flutter than the more flexible structure of the monoplane. Later, much research was devoted to flutter and it became a rare occurrence with the benefits from high-speed wind tunnels and computers. The modern monoplane has nothing in common with the early wire-braced structure as the wing is now usually a hollow metal cantilever in which is stored fuel, landing gear, and much else. But after those early disasters, the Minister in charge of aviation, General Seely, decided to ban monoplanes after consulting with Fred Green, and the Assistant Superintendent at Farnborough, and myself.

On the human side, there is no doubt that these disasters had a definite if only temporary effect on the few of us flying at that time. I was fortunate in that fear never really threatened to spoil my pleasure and enthusiasm, except when I was very tired or unfit. Then I found that the pleasure and satisfaction could be tainted with apprehension, and my imagination got to work, picturing all sorts of unpleasant, and unlikely, things happening: the sound and sight of a wing suddenly folding up, or of a fractured propeller blade tearing the engine out. The occasion of the monoplane crashes was an extreme example. It was crass stupidity to send pilots off on an icy morning flight, often of some hours, without so much as a cup of tea beforehand, but that was normal practice at the time, and I was feeling chilled all through, rather weak and with a vacuum inside when I landed beside the wreckage with its two battered and dead bodies. It was perhaps hardly surprising that, although I am not susceptible to fainting, I came nearer to doing so then than at any other time in my life. Afterwards I had some sharp words with Brooke-Popham who was my passenger during the manœuvres, and in future tea and biscuits were provided.

But the most unpleasant experience I had in nearly fifty years of flying occurred twelve months later, in the autumn of 1913. I was due to do a test flight on a R.E.1 biplane at Farnborough. It was the first of its type and an improvement on the B.E.2, but did not possess the stability of the B.E.2C. It was early morning and a fog started to spread over the land. Today it seems strange that the extreme dangers of flying in fog were not realized in the early days. Another interesting fact is that pilots often climbed through fog or a few thousand feet of cloud without losing control although at that time, some two years later than the earlier experience of cloud flying I have described, there were no blind flying instruments. We had a crude air speed indicator in the form of coloured liquid in a U-tube, an altimeter and a compass. There were, of course, no parachutes. I have discussed this matter of flying through cloud with other early pilots, and it seems that it was largely psychological—as long as we did not realize the danger all was well, but when it was fully realized due to an increasing number of fatal accidents, no one could fly through cloud without apprehension of losing control.

On the morning of the test I decided to take off 'to see if the weather was good enough'. Directly the wheels left the ground I could see nothing but thick fog and knew it would be impossible to return to the aerodrome. The great airship shed was straight ahead, so I turned left to avoid hitting it, and flew on until a tree loomed up very close in front of the nose. I just had time to pull the stick back and jump over it. Chimney pots on houses suddenly appeared in the same way and had to be 'jumped'. After about ten minutes of this nightmare I realized it was far too risky, so I started to climb steadily. By this time I understood, as never before, the meaning of fear. There was no question of stopping to think things out, and I knew I just had to go on, concentrating all my attention on the crucial necessity of maintaining a safe speed above stalling point at the correct angle of ascent. In flying 'blind' without proper instruments the rudder is, I think, the most likely control to lead you into trouble, for there can be a false sense of turning to right or left which leads naturally to the tendency to correct with the rudder bar. This must be rigidly resisted or a spin may result. As I climbed through the fog it gradually became more luminous and I emerged at three thousand feet into brilliant sunlight and an azure sky, with a level sea of dazzling white cloud extending to all horizons. But this was a false paradise, for I was a prisoner in this wide and lovely world above the fog-bound earth. I did what most of us instinctively do in times of great stress; I prayed hard. I tried to decide in which direction to fly, and, knowing that the more open country lay to the west, steered in that direction by compass. Climbing steadily for about fifteen minutes, I occupied myself with calculations as to how long the fuel would last and just how unpleasant the result of engine failure would be. A long and anxious period passed before I suddenly spotted in the far distance what appeared to be a very small, dark patch. As I drew nearer I saw that it was a tiny break in the cloud, and with a sudden excitement that was like a shock I dived my 'plane towards it.

There far below, as dimly perceived as the base of a deep well, was a small piece of good earth. I thrust down through it and landed in the first field I saw. My landing on the stubble was untidy but the relief of being on the ground again was overwhelming. I went to a nearby farmhouse where they gave me tea. I tried to talk normally about having a little difficulty with fog and finding a place to land. When the mist had lifted a little after waiting an hour, I was able to get back to Farnborough by flying low.

If I seem to have made much of this episode it is because it was a most frightening experience, and one which taught me a lesson about fog which I could never forget. I believe even today there are too many accidents due to low cloud, and many beginners do not realize the deadly peril of flying in fog even with the help of modern instruments. This adventure did not in the least diminish my love of flying, but the experience may have saved me from disaster in later years.

There were, however, less serious and more entertaining aspects of cloud flying. Some pilots claimed to have been in strange 'magnetic' clouds which caused the compass needle to rotate, and it was sometimes difficult to persuade them that the compass needle had been relatively still and that the aeroplane had been rotating round it, but because they were flying 'blind' they were quite unaware that they were turning. Another belief that died hard, and even today is still sometimes accepted, was the matter of turning down wind and turning up wind. It was said that turning down wind was tricky and might be dangerous. There was some truth in this, but it was only indirectly to do with the wind. In starting a turn fairly near the ground when flying *against* the wind one appears to be, and is, moving more slowly over the ground and one may tend to increase speed; when flying *with* the wind one appears to be, and is, moving faster over the ground and therefore tends to reduce speed before turning. This may be dangerous because one is judging speed relative to the ground instead of relative to the air.

This problem is simplified by imagining a sphere of air, say, five miles in diameter, and in this sphere an aeroplane is flying at 60 m.p.h. Now imagine this whole sphere of air moving over the ground at 60 m.p.h. as happens in a gale, the aeroplane and pilot will not be aware of this movement unless the ground is visible, but in one direction (with the wind) the aeroplane will be doing 120 m.p.h. over the ground, and if it turns 'against the wind' will be stationary over the ground but still flying at 60 m.p.h. relative to the air—which is all that matters as regards safety. The obvious answer is to fly by air speed indicator which always gives the speed through the air and has nothing to do with the speed over the ground. Although it does not eliminate the air speed indicator, one of the simplest and therefore most reliable instruments of all time is a piece of string about twelve inches long, one end tied to any point projecting about six inches on the upper part of the nose of the aeroplane. In straight flight the string trails out horizontally, in a flat turn it is blown sideways indicating 'yaw', and at varying speeds its angle with the horizontal varies. At least one famous pilot, John Cunningham, still adds this simple device to the mass of complex modern instruments on all Comets.

Another experience at Farnborough that might have ended disastrously occurred while testing an unusual design of aeroplane, officially named the F.E.3. It had a single tail boom from the rear of the pusher propeller, braced to the wings. The engine was in the nose, and drive to the propeller was by a long shaft and gearing. I was about to do the first flight, opened the throttle and had just got clear of the ground when a large sheet of engine cowling came adrift and flashed past me and into the propeller. One of the four blades was broken off short, and the out-of-balance forces set up were terrific. The whole cockpit vibrated and shook so violently that my hand was shaken off the throttle and vision became no more than a grey blur. For perhaps a second I was completely paralysed and incapable of any action, even to save my life. An instinct for self-preservation, however, at last caused my hand to reach out for the throttle lever, and I was able to slow the engine to a 'tick over'. I returned to the peace and security of the earth, which was luckily not far away, as quickly as possible. This F.E.3 type never came up to expectations and was eventually abandoned.

*

Looking back now to the 1910 to 1914 period of flying, when we were still feeling our way and no one had much idea about the destination anyway, it is remarkable how brief was the period between the time when we were satisfied at being able merely to remain aloft and land without damage, and the stirrings of ambition to accomplish something more spectacular. I think the idea of performing aerobatics occurred to most of us almost as soon as we could spare some concentration from the simple act of flying. One of the first to try was the Frenchman, Pégoud, who did some looping and inverted flying at Hendon above an excited crowd around 1912 or 1913, in a Blériot with special bracing. At Farnborough, even before this time, Norman Spratt, Winfield Smith and I often talked about looping the loop, but thought it unwise to ask O'Gorman for permission in case it should put him into the difficult position of refusing. At Farnborough, anything relating to aerobatics was considered in the class of a circus stunt, and the official attitude was that anything like Pégoud's goings-on at Hendon was rather too *infra dig.* for a Government factory to indulge in. So we decided to try it first and talk afterwards.

I took out one of my own B.E.2s and climbed up to a good height. I knew that it was a manoeuvre that could not be tried gradually, for anything like a half-hearted effort with too little speed could result in the 'plane falling sideways from the vertical with loss of control. At three thousand feet I levelled the 'plane out and opened up to full throttle, at the same time pushing forward the stick so that I went into a shallow dive. As the angle of dive increased, so the speed rose, although it was a matter of judgement as the air speed indicator lagged in its recording, and was unreliable anyway. When I thought I was travelling about as fast as the 'plane's structure could reasonably be expected to stand, I pulled the stick back firmly and at once began to feel the pressure against my seat. For the first time in my life I had come near to a black-out, caused by the body's blood being forced from the head, before I saw that I was climbing steeply. I held the stick in the same position, against all my instincts, soon the earth's horizon that had previously been behind me came into sight—upside down of course. Within less than a second, my 'plane was again in a steep dive, and all I had to do to regain the horizontal and my previous course was to pull back on the stick. It had been a strange and interesting experience, and had proved easy to accomplish.

All this sounds mild and simple enough now, but there were several factors which made it a shade more hazardous in those days. The most important was the inadequate power, which naturally narrowed the margin of safety in all manœuvres: while today, of course, a jet fighter with its tremendous power can make light of a loop straight off the ground. There was also the unknown factor of structural and mechanical safety when inverted. Nor did we have either parachute or safety harness. Later, a thin lap strap was provided for inverted flying, but we discovered that in a well-judged loop the 'plane and the pilot had to withstand very little negative load; or, put another way, the load was always on the pilot's behind and there was never any risk of falling out even when on top of the loop.

Looping the loop, inverted flying and other aerobatics became quite 'the thing' just before the outbreak of the First World War. Looping was not really dangerous, except in aircraft that were dangerous anyway, and there were few accidents. But for some time it was classed as quite a sensational evolution, and there were many stories about it, some of them apocryphal. For instance, there was the R.F.C. pilot who carried out rather a poor one, turned round in his cockpit to see how his passenger had taken it and found the seat empty. There were also the two Frenchmen who took their 'plane up to a very high speed in the dive to be sure of getting round, and caused the wings to tear off the nacelle. As they hurtled on in their wingless nacelle, the pilot turned to his passenger, hands lifted from the useless controls and spread wide, and shrugged. *C'est la vie!*

Spinning, however, was in a different class altogether from looping, and was a dangerous and mysterious involuntary evolution right up to 1915. I have had only one flying crash worthy of that name, and that was caused by a spin, in March 1913 at Farnborough. The aeroplane was B.S.1, a small single-seater scout, the first of its type, fitted with the double row fourteen-cylinder one-hundred-horse-power Gnome engine. This machine has since been referred to as the prototype of all single-seat fighters. Aerodynamic knowledge was limited at that time, and in making the drawings I relied largely on scaling down the successful B.E.2. This method was good enough for wings and tail-plane but not for rudder which looked obviously too small when the machine was assembled, and I arranged for a rudder of greater area to be put in hand. I did not think the small rudder would lead to any serious trouble, but might not be sufficiently effective in sharp turns. I did the first test flight with the small rudder and noticed that big rudder angles were required to correct a turn. In doing a rather sharper turn than usual the aeroplane suddenly took charge and went into a spinning turn which full opposite rudder movement failed to halt. As I was below a hundred feet there was no hope of getting out of the spin, which luckily was fairly 'flat' when we hit the ground. I remember the sensation due to centrifugal force of being pressed hard against the side of the cockpit during the spin, and knew nothing more until dragged from the wreckage. The chief damage I suffered was a broken jaw and the loss of many teeth (later found in the wreckage and kindly returned in an envelope by a mechanic) and some bruises, but the aeroplane was a total wreck. While recovering in the Cambridge Hospital at Aldershot I had a visit from one of the technical people from the Factory who said, with a certain note of triumph, that they had made extensive calculations and the results proved that the rudder was too small. I tried to show interest. The aeroplane was reconstructed—with a larger rudder—and I did a lot of flying with it before it was sent to France on war service.

Mervyn O'Gorman also came to see me at the hospital and kindly brought a gramophone and a pile of records. But I think I most appreciated a book by H. G. Wells which he gave me. On the title page was written:

'To G. de Havilland from M.O'G.
In memory of an aeroplane
92—50—900.'

The figures referred to the performance we had measured: 92 miles per hour top speed, 50 miles per hour slow speed, and nine hundred feet per minute, climb. The climb was phenomenal for those days. I appreciated the words on the title page more than the contents of the book.

That was an involuntary spin, of course. The voluntary spin, however, comes under the heading of Aerobatics and is today thoroughly understood; but in those early days the spin was a difficult condition to correct and caused many fatal crashes. Briefly, spinning is caused by trying to make

90

a turn when safe flying speed has been lost and the 'plane stalls. Autorotation then occurs and the aeroplane rotates about a point near its centre. Recovery can be made provided there is sufficient height so that the 'plane can be dived to regain speed, at the same time ruddering against the turn. Too small a fin and rudder makes recovery more difficult. In fact, the danger from spins continued right up to the end of the war, and remains to this day a potential danger if the pilot makes the unforgivable error of losing flying speed at an insufficient height for recovery by diving. This applies as much to the giant airliner as to the cheapest light 'plane, and a fatal crash is almost always the result.

Recently a controversy about spinning in 1916 has arisen, with articles by Wing Commander Norman Macmillan and correspondence in the journal *Aeronautics*. Lord Cherwell—then Dr. Lindemann of the Royal Aircraft Factory—figures prominently in this controversy, which is likely to continue indefinitely because it can never be completely resolved. Around 1915 Lindemann became interested in the problem of the involuntary spin, worked out a theory and apparently decided to put it to practical test. By then at least two pilots, Sir Vernon Brown and Brooke, knew how to recover from a spin, and as early as August 1912 during the military Aeroplane Trials on Salisbury Plain I had watched Wilfred Parke recover from an accidental spin.

It is claimed by some that Lindemann obtained permission from O'Gorman to learn to fly and *within three weeks* went up on a B.E.2 and did spins and recoveries! One of the main points in the controversy is to obtain firm evidence of the date when it happened. Over thirty years later when nearly eighty years old O'Gorman suggested it took place in 1916. I found O'G's memory relating to Farnborough days was often at fault or non-existent, and feel it quite possible that he was confusing Lindemann with Goodden, the chief test pilot, who did spin tests at Farnborough in

91

1916. O'Gorman's references to Lindemann, incidentally, were far from complimentary, but he admitted that he was an able physicist. It is said that Lindemann had a 'meticulous' memory, and 'quite exceptional powers of memory', and yet when asked by someone about his spinning experiences at a later date he said: 'I really cannot remember any details about my spinning experiments', and he does not even mention spinning in his memoirs. This was said to be due to his 'deep modesty'. This 'deep modesty' prevented his suggested discoveries connected with spinning being generally and quickly known as they should have been in order to save young pilots from fatal errors. 'Sublime courage' has also been attributed to Lindemann for going up to a safe height and doing spins. This extravagant term was surely more applicable to those young pilots who, after a very few hours' flying, were fighting enemy aircraft in France while being shot at both from the ground and the air.

Major F. M. Green, who was closely in touch with Lindemann at Farnborough, puts the matter in sounder perspective when he says, 'I do not think it quite fair to rob Lindemann of his contributions to the problems of spinning . . . Major Goodden was an exceptionally good and experienced pilot and was my authority on aeroplane flight behaviour. He certainly used to do all sorts of aerobatics which must have included spinning . . . Lindemann worked out a theory of spinning far enough to encourage him to experiment in the air. This he did, and I believe had some success, but I cannot remember exactly what he reported. I do not think this had any immediate result in giving guidance in all conditions of spin, nor, I think, did it make much impression on Goodden.'

*

Before the outbreak of the 1914 War my job at Farnborough had come to an end, to my regret. In January 1914 the Aeronautical Inspection Directorate—or A.I.D.—had come into being as an independent organization for the inspection of all aircraft and engines. I was offered the position of Inspector of Aircraft, under the Chief Inspector, Colonel Fulton, and, much as I disliked the idea, pressure from high up made it difficult for me to refuse. I did at least still have the enjoyment and satisfaction from flying, but I felt miserable and wasted at being cut off from all design work, particularly as I felt that, with such 'planes as the B.E.2, I was really getting somewhere.

My release from this position came at last through the person of George Holt Thomas, who had formed the Aircraft Manufacturing Company, or Airco, and was often at Farnborough. Thomas was a tall, lean, good-looking man who always dressed well and affected a short beard of unusual cut. His father was a newspaper owner, and had started, among others, the *Daily Graphic*. He was far-sighted, extremely able and possessed a knowledge of business only equalled by his ignorance of engineering. Flying in all its aspects had engrossed his considerable talents from the earliest days, and he had persuaded Paulhan, the French pilot, to come over from France with his Farman to enter for the London–Manchester flight, which of course he won. Until our association, he had built for his company Farman biplanes under licence from the French company, and had done extremely well.

One day when Holt Thomas was at Farnborough on business I decided to take the plunge. 'Have you ever thought of having your own design department and making your own aeroplanes instead of making do with other people's designs?'

He thought about this for a moment, and then asked me with a smile. 'Why do you ask?'

'For the good reason that I want to get back to designing,' I said directly. 'I was almost forced to take this A.I.D. job, and I hate it and want to go back to my old love.'

'It's worth thinking about,' Thomas told me encouragingly. 'Why not come up to my office in London where we can discuss it without interruption?'

This talk went off excellently. He thought my idea an admirable one, and was willing to give me the job as designer and pilot to his company with increased salary. All I had to do was to hand in my resignation. This, as I suspected, was to be a most unpleasant business, mostly because the man concerned at the War Office was Sir David Henderson, a most overbearing man.

As I had anticipated, Henderson took my suggestion of resignation very badly and became quite angry. 'You know perfectly well that the A.I.D. is a new and important organization,' he told me, 'and I think you are letting us down and being thoughtless and impulsive. You were in it from the start, and there would have been good prospects of advancement.'

I told him that my mind was made up. 'I'm sorry, but my one ambition is to continue design work and flying. I don't care for inspection work and I'm sure I'll never be really efficient at it.'

I was thankful to breathe the free, fairly pure air of Whitehall again after that. My Civil Service days were over, and already my mind was humming with plans in the exciting field of aircraft design.

CHAPTER SIX

THE FIRST AIRCRAFT IN WAR

'THE said Geoffrey de Havilland,' ran my agreement with Holt Thomas dated May 23, 1914, 'will design and supervise the construction of such aeroplanes as the company may require and will pilot any such aeroplanes designed by him . . . By way of remuneration for his services under this agreement the Company will pay to the said Geoffrey de Havilland a salary of six hundred pounds per annum . . . and a commission of fifty pounds per aeroplane on the first twenty of all such aeroplanes sold in any year, and a commission of twenty-five pounds per aeroplane on all such aeroplanes exceeding the number of twenty.' The agreement was to last 'one year certain from the second day of July 1914'.

As soon as my notice had expired, I left Farnborough thankfully and moved my family to Edgware, where we bought a small house, and later a Model 'T' Ford car, which, being our first new car, was tenderly cared for and housed in a farm building nearby. We used it only at weekends, and I always rode to work on a second-hand bicycle. Louie liked the life at Edgware better, too.

It was wonderful to be working on the design side again, and under a brilliantly clever as well as a kind and likeable man. I looked forward to a prosperous and creative future with Airco. But of course all these cherished dreams and ambitions were shattered by Britain's declaration of war with Germany in August.

When at Farnborough I had joined the Royal Flying

Corps Reserve, and had for three years flown on Army manœuvres. As soon as war became inevitable I was called back to Farnborough, ordered into uniform and attached to the Reserve. Then I went up before a medical board, who found me fit for flying but, because the effects of my crash had not entirely disappeared, this was limited to home duties only. Without more ado—and without any kind of disciplinary instruction or drill—I was posted in August to Montrose on the east coast of Scotland as an officer on war duty. From this little flying field two of us, Sergeant Carr and myself, were to protect British shipping from the German U-boats between Aberdeen and the Firth of Forth. We were provided with two old 50-h.p. Blériot monoplanes for this purpose, each with a top speed of between forty and fifty m.p.h., a short range, and a total absence of guns, bombs, wireless or parachutes. Neither Sergeant Carr nor I would have cared to distinguish a German battleship from a British cruiser, let alone a U-boat from a Royal Navy submarine. However, we carried out our curious missions obediently and without question—as did so many others at the early stages of both world wars—Sergeant Carr patrolling Aberdeen to Montrose, while I took Montrose to the Firth of Forth. Luckily we never saw a thing.

Towards the end of the month I suppose someone woke up to the fact that a man who had designed several quite useful warplanes already was risking his neck daily piloting an obsolete foreign machine on abortive missions over the sea up north. By the end of August I was back at Farnborough, but three months passed before the creaky wheels of bureaucracy turned to release me and I could go back to the drawing office at Hendon. Even then I was still nominally in the service, was supposed to wear uniform and was subject to immediate recall, which had an unsettling effect on my work and added to the general strain.

At Airco I quickly built up a design team and got down

to serious work, starting first on a tractor biplane. However, the War Office soon made it clear that what it wanted from us was a pusher machine (with the propeller behind) in order to give the gunner a clear field of fire. Later, of course, a method of firing a machine-gun between the blades of a tractor airscrew was developed, and the pusher machine went out of fashion. This pusher was to be a two-seater, and became known at Airco as the D.H.1. No one has ever been able to discover how my initials came to be adopted, and before anything became official I suggested to Holt Thomas that we should at least prefix our aircraft D.H.T. to embody both our initials. But it was already too late. Like a school nickname, it had come to stay and nothing could change it.

We built two or three of these D.H.1s, which flew quite well, but before serious production could begin the demand from the War Office changed to a single-seat fighter with a higher performance to counteract the formidable German Fokker. The need was obviously urgent and we worked on the D.H.2 night and day, having the first model in the air by July 1915. It was powered by a 100-h.p. Mono-Gnome rotary engine and carried a single Lewis gun in the nose of the cockpit. The D.H.2 fulfilled its role against the Fokker satisfactorily and went into such large scale production that the works and offices had to be substantially enlarged. Some four hundred D.H.2s went into service with the R.F.C. The D.H.3 was a twin-engined bomber with a top speed of about 100 m.p.h. and sufficient range to bomb Berlin, but before it could be made in any numbers official policy changed again, turning against the twin-engined machine and ours had to be put aside for the time being in favour of a fast single-engined day bomber. The German Fokker E1 had by then appeared on the Western Front with a gun interrupter gear, which allowed the pilot to fire forward through the tractor propeller and gave him a great advantage. A similar Constantinesco gear became

available to the Allies soon afterwards, and I could therefore return to my earlier ideas for the tractor machine
which had been my first choice when I had joined Airco.
We now also had higher powered engines. We began
work at once and with enthusiasm on the D.H.4, this being
an orthodox biplane of wood construction but of high aerodynamic qualities. A single machine-gun fired forward
through the propeller, operated by the pilot, who acted
also as bomb-aimer, while behind the petrol tank at his
rear, and connected by speaking tube, was the observer
who had the use of a defensive Lewis gun. Like the
Mosquito of the Second World War, the D.H. 4 was faster
than any other contemporary bomber and could hold its
own against most fighters, too. Early types had a six-
cylinder B.H.P. engine, but this was later replaced by the
twelve-cylinder Rolls-Royce Eagle.

The D.H.4 formed the basis of the design for the D.H.9
and 9A, both of which, like the 4, went into very large
production both in Britain and in America. The significant
success of the 4 and its derivatives was, I believe, due to
the same reasons that make all 'good' aeroplanes, and
which applied equally to the later Moth. These are simplicity, right size, cleanness in design, and of course, a
very reliable engine. The value of simplicity is to be found
in weight saving, ease of production, reliability and lower
cost. Size is governed chiefly by the power of the chosen
engine, and if the size is right, the aeroplane becomes more
versatile in use—again exemplified more recently in the
Mosquito. In a few cases the 4 and 9A had trouble due to
tail flutter. This happened at high speed, when diving on a
target or getting out of control in cloud and emerging in a
high-speed dive. The first 9A developed flutter when
diving on a target at Martlesham test station. Luckily we
were able to examine the wreckage and prove that the tail
had failed, followed by the wings in down load. The
modification to strengthen the tail plane was straight-

forward and easily made to all existing 4s, 9s and 9As. The American-built D.H.4s were used long after the war, and Charles Lindbergh flew them on aerial postal service for some time. The last war aeroplane we produced at Hendon was the D.H.10, a re-design of the D.H.3, fitted with two Rolls-Royce Eagle engines, but before it was ready to go into service the war was over. By 1917 we were producing over three hundred aircraft a month, and we had grown from a small works to a large factory covering several acres and employing several thousand workers.

*

While working as chief designer under Holt Thomas at Airco, I built up a team of men around me who were later to form the nucleus of the de Havilland Company. They were a remarkable and well-knit company without whose devotion and co-operation over a period of many years I could have achieved nothing in the world of aeronautics. Because we remained together as a united team for so long and until the time for retirement came for us in turn—and indeed they are all alive and good friends of mine today—I should mention them at this point.

First must come Charles Walker. It was early in 1915 that I received a letter from Walker who asked me if we could make use of his services in aircraft design during the war period as he felt he had the qualities and was prevented from joining up due to an old disability. He had had a very thorough engineering education, both civil and mechanical, three years with a large Tyneside firm, was an A.M.I.C.E. and had always been interested in aeronautics. I liked the tone of his letter and asked him to come for a talk. I was at once impressed by his personality and sincerity.

'Do you know anything about the stressing of aircraft?' I asked him.

'Not as such,' Walker replied, 'but I have done a good

deal of stress work generally, using the latest graphical methods, and I should have thought that these applied to aircraft structures.'

When we began discussing salary, he said, 'Wouldn't it be best if I came for no salary for a time, and you could then decide whether to take me on for a further period on normal terms?'

Charles Walker proved to be not only exceptionally able in his work, but one of the most lovable personalities I have known, and today he is one of my oldest and best friends. One of his endearing habits is always to see and accentuate what is good in a person and to belittle their faults, and without being in any way extreme he can almost always point to some good in a situation that seems at first sight to be nothing but troublesome and difficult. He can even point out the totally hidden virtues of the English weather. His technical work, largely connected with stressing and also with aerodynamics, was always an asset of great value, and as well he has contributed an indefinable something towards the high standing of our company.

Charles Walker's sense of humour is precious and unique. In his rather slow, deep voice and with quite a serious expression, he will launch a surprising remark or statement, and I still find it hard to know whether he believes it himself or not. For instance, there is his tale of how, in his motor cycle days, he had a crash and turned many somersaults. Before the crash he had been feeling far from well, but when he got up from the ground afterwards he felt completely all right again.

'Have you a theory to explain it?' (as he always has theories for everything), I asked him.

'Yes, I'm sure it was due to a sort of rough massage I got when somersaulting along the road, it seemed to loosen things up,' he replied.

I asked him once if he knew a certain aviation personality and he said, 'Yes, he often comes to see me and I have known him for twelve years, but have never spoken to him.'

'Can you explain a bit more?' I asked.

He said: 'Well, he likes talking and is talking as he enters my room, he talks non-stop for an hour and leaves talking, so I have never been able to speak to him.'

Walker's knowledge on general subjects is phenomenal, and he had on many occasions put me and others on the right track with a quiet word of advice. The Walkers suffered a great tragedy during the Second World War. They had an only child, David, who was killed in the Royal Air Force practising night flying. David was a talented and lovable boy, and his leaning was strongly towards music rather than flying. He had an unusually fine voice and was training to become a singer. When war came he decided to join the Royal Air Force rather than the other services because of his family association with flying, but I doubt if he was really keen, and feel that he showed real courage in his determination to become a pilot. David and Charles had been very close companions, and it was a cruel blow to both his parents.

Wilfred E. Nixon was at the Royal Aircraft Factory at Farnborough when I was there but we seldom met as he was on the financial-clerical side. We both joined Holt Thomas at Hendon, not by design, but more due to a mutual friend at Farnborough, Hugh Burroughes, who joined Holt Thomas at Airco and became General Manager and Director. Burroughes persuaded Nixon to come along, too, and he remained with us through the war.

Afterwards, when we decided to form our own company at Stag Lane, Nixon was obviously the man to take charge of the financial side. Since then he has held the position of Secretary, Financial Director and eventually Chairman, and the company has grown during that time into a great and complex enterprise. I have to confess that figures,

101

finance and business affairs have always defeated me. At board meetings there would often be charts of figures interspersed with strange words or signs. I would stare intently at these for a good time and then look up, trying hard to appear as if I understood. If they had been Chinese they couldn't have meant less to me. It was difficult to tell even if we were doing well or badly, because Nixon had a way of making us feel things were going badly, and then at the end of the year he would spring a surprise because he had found we had really done rather well. From our modest beginnings in 1920 until the space age forty years later, the de Havilland enterprise expanded beyond anything even dimly imagined. The enormous increase in output during the war of aircraft, engines, propellers and much else, and then the difficult return to conditions of uneasy peace, have demanded continuous control and sound judgement on the part of Nixon and his chosen staff, and it is a measure of his business and financial ability that he made these changes possible and successful. In private life he is interested in birds and natural history generally, and is fond of gardening. He lost his eldest son when flying early in the war, and has had several cruel family bereavements. He retired in 1959 after forty-nine years' association with aviation, nearly forty years being with our company. Although we did not always see eye to eye, I have the greatest admiration for Nixon and his work, which has little glamour and is seldom adequately recognized.

Francis St. Barbe was in charge of sales at Airco before I arrived; and sales remained his special charge through the First World War, all the fluctuations in our fortunes from 1919 to 1939, through World War II and right up to his retirement in 1961. St. Barbe is not a technical man, and is only interested in design and construction as it affects the saleability of a product. His genius was shown in his business ability and in the world wide sales organization he tirelessly built up without giving a thought to fame or fortune.

St. Barbe can be very exacting and, at times, rather ruthless in support of something which he feels requires drastic action. He has contributed as much as anyone to the success the de Havilland Company achieved since it was founded over forty years ago.

While Frank Hearle was still at Farnborough with me he was offered and accepted a better job as Works Foreman at the Deperdussin Aircraft Company at Highgate, but the company failed a year later. Hearle then joined Vickers at Erith, building a few aircraft for the Royal Flying Corps. When war started in 1914 he was given the job of starting up a Vickers factory at Weybridge and building B.E.2 biplanes. In 1917 he was sent by Vickers to America to try to get the Vickers Scout adopted there, but this did not work out. On his return he joined Airco at Hendon where I was designing and took charge of the Experimental Shop.

All these men at Airco were founder members of the de Havilland Company. Frank Halford came to us later, as chief designer in the Engine Division, but I had known him many years earlier, first at Farnborough, where he was a sergeant in the Royal Flying Corps before 1914, and then as the designer (with Beardmore and Pullinger—hence the initials) of the B.H.P. engine that powered the early D.H.4s. Halford was a brilliant engineer who turned his hand to a wide variety of engine work, including racing cars at Brooklands. His enthusiasm was unbounded and his exceptional driving force resulted in his getting things done with the least possible delay. For a long time he showed the same fighting spirit in overcoming a serious throat illness, only to die later, and quite suddenly, of coronary thrombosis.

As aircraft production at Airco rose steadily and rapidly during the 1914–18 War, it became quite impossible for me to stick to my previous rule that I should carry out all the testing myself at Hendon. So I engaged two pilots who remained with us almost to the end. The first of these and our Chief Pilot was B. C. Hucks, a very likeable man and a fine pilot, who had also had engineering training at Thornycrofts and some air fighting in France before being invalided home. As a test and demonstration pilot he was outstanding, and he could put a D.H.4 into evolutions never seen before. On one occasion our chief engine man asked for a flight in a D.H.4. Hucks put it through all his well-known spectacular manœuvres and we saw a hand frequently waving from the passenger's cockpit, apparently expressing enjoyment. But when Hucks landed we found a huddled figure in the passenger's cockpit in a state of near collapse. Apparently he had a slight heart weakness and thought he was going to 'pass out'.

Hucks invented several very practical devices and they always worked. The best known was the 'Hucks Starter'. Aero engines still had to be started by the dangerous method of swinging the propeller, as there were as yet no self-starters. Hucks used a standard Model 'T' Ford chassis and arranged it to drive a long, overhead horizontal shaft with a universal joint so that the end of the shaft could be engaged with a suitable fixing on the aero engine propeller shaft. It disengaged automatically when the engine started. This clever improvisation was ordered by the Air Ministry and every Royal Air Force aerodrome had its Hucks Starter.

Other test pilots were Clement Gresswell, who later became aerodrome manager, and W. Birchenough, a good pilot and, like Gresswell, a motor-car enthusiast. The pilots at Hendon during the 1914 War were a cheerful lot, and I often walked down to the aerodrome as a relief from constant drawing office work.

Other welcome reliefs from the quite severe pressure of work at Hendon were provided by Holt Thomas himself,

104

who began the excellent practice of inviting three or four of his staff at a time to lunch at the Royal Automobile Club, where we could relax and talk over informally anything that was on our minds, whether it related to work or anything else. In this congenial atmosphere we drank the best liqueurs and champagne in tankards, and were offered the best cigars.

*

One reason why I had to give up some of the testing work at Hendon was my insistence that I should make frequent flights to France to get first-hand information from the front line squadrons on any technical troubles our aircraft might be suffering from. These visits were useful in another way, too. I learnt much from the pilots on the spot, and I usually went out with senior R.F.C. officers, perhaps General Sykes, or his successor 'Boom' Trenchard, and discussed directly with them new types of aircraft that might be required in the future.

Trenchard in particular was a fascinating character. He was not a technical man, but was always reasonable and helpful in discussion. I had a very high regard for him and have always thought of him as one of the great men of his time. I had known him slightly a year or two before the war when I was in the Royal Flying Corps Reserve on manœuvres. At the end of the manœuvres, in 1912 or 1913, I had a note from Captain Trenchard, who was in charge of stores, asking if I knew anything about some Army blankets that were missing. I replied rather tersely that I knew nothing about the blankets and had given mine in.

Trenchard soon became Major, and after some lapse of time I remember meeting him in an office at Farnborough at the beginning of the 1914 War when he was in charge of a small local section of the Royal Flying Corps. He admitted that he did not enjoy the job and wanted to go

105

overseas. If he wanted to do something he usually did it, and I was not surprised, when I next saw him, that he said, with a note of triumph: 'I'm going overseas next week.' Not long after that I met him in France fairly frequently where he was in his element and could give of his best. Later on he arranged and got authority to form the Independent Air Force, entirely under his control, for bombing behind the lines. Our D.H.4s and 9s were used mainly for this purpose and did well.

Trenchard hated writing letters, and when he did they were as short as possible. I therefore value highly a letter I was surprised to get from him about the first D.H.4. It is headed 'Headquarters, R.A.F., 20th October 1916.'

> 'Thank you for your letter of 17th on the subject of the de Havilland 4. As a reconnaissance fighter I think it will be a first rate machine, but I do not think it is entirely suitable for bomb dropping. For a large machine it is extremely handy to fly. It is quick on turns with very sensitive fore and aft controls and has a very large range of speed. The criticisms I have made have been sent home to General Brancker. I also approve very much of your suggested alterations.
>
> Yours sincerely,
> H. Trenchard.'

I cannot remember the 'alterations' mentioned in his letter, but probably bigger tanks were fitted. The D.H.4 had not yet been tried as a bomber, and I think Trenchard may have been in error, because it did a great deal of bombing later on and was considered very successful in this role.

Trenchard had as his secretary Maurice Baring, the writer and poet, who was always within call with his note-book—('Baring, make a note of this . . .'). Boom gave him plenty to do and was rather exacting, so Baring devised subtle 'punishments' from time to time. Boom hated draughts in his car and usually had the windows shut, but one day when he was not looking Baring broke a window by a sharp jab with his elbow and then apologized for his clumsiness. Boom had to suffer in the draught while Baring had the satisfaction of inflicting 'punishment'.

In spite of very few opinions to the contrary, and of a ruthlessness that was often needed at the time, I believe Trenchard was a most popular leader of the Royal Flying Corps, and later of the Royal Air Force. At times our casualties were high, but being above all a fighter, he attacked more fiercely than ever. I remember an occasion when we were trying to build an aircraft that was more ambitious than usual in performance and he said: 'Good luck to it, and if it doesn't quite achieve the performance there need be no hard words, you are aiming high, and that means taking some risk, so don't worry.' These encouraging words were in strong contrast with the normal official attitude in such situations. When he later became Marshal of the Royal Air Force, Lord Trenchard, G.C.B., G.C.V.O., D.S.O., I often recalled his concern over the army blankets.

I knew Tizard well. Henry Tizard (later Sir Henry Tizard, F.R.S.) flew in the 1914–18 War and was appointed to the test station at Martlesham Heath. Until his time, the testing of aircraft had been somewhat haphazard, and in the early war years reports were often dependent on the pilot's state of mind at the time, and even on whether he was still suffering from a hangover as a result of last night's party, when of course there was nothing good to be heard about the 'plane. Tizard changed all this by putting test flying on a sound scientific basis with instrument recordings and a whole range of standards of accuracy. Tizard later held high positions in aeronautical science, but I will always remember him for his work in lifting test flying out of the dangerous rut into which it had understandably fallen. In my own case there were no instruments available when I started and I was too keen on actual flying to bother much about them until they became a real necessity in blind flying and other conditions.

*

Two important and closely related things happened to me during the closing stages of the first war: I became quite 'well off', and I suffered from a nervous breakdown. My 1914 agreement with Holt Thomas had not taken into account the sudden acceleration of production and sales always brought about by a war, and I naturally suggested to him that it should be revised. But Holt Thomas brushed this suggestion aside. 'This is normally a chancy business,' he said, 'and now that the work is vitally necessary it is only legitimate to do reasonably well out of it.' When I had first signed up with Airco I remembered saying to Louie that it might not be long before we had a thousand pounds in the bank, when we could begin to feel secure. But a few months later I received a cheque for £1,500, and we felt really well off. As more aircraft were delivered more money came in until I began to develop an attitude towards money that I had always suspected had lain dormant in me—that it was a very necessary evil that brought with it irksome responsibility and a high nuisance value. There have been times since then when the money has been quite short, and others when it has flowed fairly freely, but I have never been able to summon up much interest in it, and think I can fairly say that I am not an acquisitive man. The sheer nuisance of possessing a lot of money has always seemed to me to outweigh the advantages of great affluence. However, in 1915 I did not stretch this to the point of refusing royalties due to me, and Louie and I decided to look for a larger house. We found one only a mile away, still in Edgware; hideous Edwardian outside, but spacious inside, and the garden with its large trees and a fair-sized natural pond was a great improvement. We built a garage for two cars, sold the Ford and bought a big six-cylinder Buick. Our third son, John, was born there, and he and Louie were the only members of the family to escape the great 'flu epidemic that raged through the Continent and Britain in 1918 and 1919.

Domestically the war was a quiet one, and we suffered as a family no more and no less than any other from the food scarcity; although Louie did, against all regulations, without my knowledge build up a fine store of sugar against an emergency. She then read all about people being heavily fined and even jailed for hoarding, at once got into a panic and asked me what she should do. At that time it was worse than having a store of dynamite in the house, and I tried to think of a safe place for it, even contemplating sinking it in the pond in a rubber bag. In the end I resorted to seeking advice from our next door neighbour, a good friend who was also a solicitor in the City. He said he would be glad to look after it for us, just to relieve Louie's anxiety of course. Louie was overjoyed, and the solicitor was true to his word: we never saw the sugar again.

However, the illicit sugar hoard was the least of my worries. Ever since the end of 1914 I had been under extreme pressure, and by mid-1918 I realized suddenly that I had been feeling physically and mentally exhausted for some time. The inevitable climax to this state, when it came, was severe. Far less about nerve exhaustion was understood then than now, but a nerve specialist insisted on several months' complete rest in a nursing home. I recalled the periods of depression of earlier days, but at least they had been only brief, whereas this was now almost continuous. With complete rest I began to recover under a kindly and understanding doctor, who pointed out that the stress of much flying long before and during the war, testing many entirely new types, all added to the concentration and strain demanded by design work had been too much for me. Recovery was gradual but sure, and in a few months work began to take on renewed interest, colour began to return to life and things gradually became normal again. After a bad breakdown there always seems to be a definite warning to 'go slow' if ever the danger point is again approached.

During an ill-advised and ghastly holiday at Brighton before going to the nursing home, I had the mistaken feeling that if we could find a pleasant place in which to live in the country I would be well. We heard of a house near Balcombe, a lovely part of Sussex. Louie and I went to see it and at once fell in love with the house, garden and surrounding country. It was all as near perfect as it could be, and I foolishly skated over the difficulty of getting to London and returning daily. We decided to buy the house and move in when I left the nursing home. But the problem of getting to and from work was just the sort of thing that could be magnified in my still weak condition at that time into a terrifying difficulty beyond solution, and after living at Balcombe for a few months the house was sold. Fortunately, Louie was able to find a suitable but ugly house in Stanmore, not far from Hendon and near to our old friends. This speeded my complete recovery, and I was able to do some of my best and most strenuous work in design and flying in the years that followed. But the illness had been a severe warning that there were definite limits beyond which I must never again trespass.

CHAPTER SEVEN

THE BIRTH OF THE COMPANY

THE aftermath of war with all its wild extravagances seems to leave an immediate legacy of slight madness in industry, above all in the aircraft industry. Airco was no exception in 1919. The directors had fantastic dreams of developments in commercial flying, with airliner links between European cities on a scale that was not approached for another thirty years. For this purpose two ex-Royal Air Force generals were engaged and designs of large and small commercial aircraft were started and expensive sales missions sent abroad. But as orders for military aircraft had suddenly stopped, and the orders for civil machines were insignificant, the company was soon in difficulties. In 1919 Airco was taken over by the Birmingham Small Arms Company who quickly made it clear that they did not wish to touch aeroplanes, and only wanted the buildings and plant. It was a sudden and sad ending. The premature dreams of a great aeronautical manufacturing company were shattered almost overnight, the generals had to go and the staff had to prepare to find other jobs.

The break-up may have been a blessing in disguise for some because it forced us to take definite action about our future. At this time we did have a small amount of work at Airco, and B.S.A. were ready for this work to be transferred to us if we were able, as we hoped, to start a small aircraft company. The 'we' I refer to were Nixon, St. Barbe, Walker, Hearle and myself. We were all of one mind about forming a small company if it could possibly be done, although at that time future prospects were as uncertain as ever. Nixon was to be Secretary and deal with finance generally, an awe-inspiring and dreadful task; St. Barbe would be Business and Sales Manager; Hearle, Works Manager; Walker Chief of Aerodynamics and Stressing; while I would deal with design with Arthur E. Hagg as head of the Drawing Office. Hagg had been with us at Airco and had shown a genius for design, although he had not had an engineering training. He later became Chief Designer, a position he held for about ten years.

Finance was the first problem, and Holt Thomas, to whom the failure of Airco was a severe blow, came forward very nobly and promised to put up £10,000. I wrote to some well-known people who were interested in aviation and to friends, but very few were prepared to risk their money, and I can hardly blame them. One of my friends found £1,000 and I found £3,000, and so, with well under £20,000 capital we started The de Havilland Aircraft Company. The Company was registered on September 25, 1920, with a working capital of £1,875, and perhaps an unwarranted degree of optimism.

The obvious site for the new venture was Stag Lane Aerodrome at Edgware, which had been a training aerodrome during the war and was only about three miles from Hendon. The two partners who owned it agreed to rent it to us. Their business of flying training had ended with the war, and their first attack of 'after war madness' was to start making chocolates, of which they knew nothing, but which left a sticky mess which we had to clear up. We were able to bring away a small technical staff from Airco as well as a small group of woodworkers, fitters, machinists and inspectors, and we also had a few good aero engine men.

The accommodation was poor. A wooden building was the main office block, divided into four small offices, one containing the telephone. This wooden 'office block', which housed the directors, their typist and the telephone, was later moved to Hatfield when we were established there

112

The motor cycle which I designed and which had some novel features: Note the unusual coiled finning on the cylinder

My first aeroplane which flew. Frank Hearle starting the engine

Louie, my
first wife,
stitching the
covering for
our first
aeroplane in
the workshop
at Fulham

The first de Havilland aeroplane which flew, photographed at Seven Barrows, Hampshire, where I learned to fly

The first of my aeroplanes which flew, doing acceptance trials at Farnborough

D.H.60 Gipsy Moth with sealed Gipsy engine, flown by Hubert Broad for twenty-four hours non-stop

My three sons *(left to right),* Peter, John and Geoffrey, discussing the tail of a Mosquito

Peter de Havilland, Geoffrey Jnr., John, Hereward and Sir Geoffrey de Havilland

Olivia de Havilland and Sir Geoffrey in Comet Cockpit

I took the photo of this old wild bull elephant at 'Treetops' in Kenya. He was ten yards away from the bottom of the ladder where I was waiting with my partly home-made camera. At first I was dead quiet, but after he had dug in the salt lick for half an hour I was talking to him in a loud voice. He moved off in a leisurely way to rejoin the herd nearby. It was a most happy and satisfying experience to have this close and apparently friendly contact with a wild elephant.

The story has a sad ending. 'My' elephant was shot a year later, for no good reason, by a so-called 'sportsman' only a mile or so away from our meeting place

Taken in the Queen Elizabeth National Park, Uganda. This hippo in its mud bath was quite unconcerned when our car broke down and we got out to investigate. He watched our efforts at repairs with interest.

The D.H.98 Mosquito war machine, of which 7,781 were built

The D.H.106, Comet 4, four Rolls-Royce Avon engines, with wing tanks for longer range

and now houses a museum for many and various exhibits, including scale models of most of our aircraft and engines and many other items of interest. The drawing office was housed in another wooden shed which leaked when it rained, and the power for the two or three machine tools was provided by a nearly worn-out gas engine. The first work of our new company at Stag Lane, was the finishing of two D.H.18s which had been started at Airco. The '18' was our first aircraft designed purely as a civil transport. It was a biplane with a roomy cabin seating eight passengers, but the pilot was still in an open cockpit at the rear of the cabin. The engine was a Napier Lion. The D.H.18 was used by the first civil transport company to be formed in England known as Air Transport and Travel, or A.T. & T. Formed by Holt Thomas, it did good service on the early civil flights to the Continent. Prior to the D.H.18, civil aircraft had been improvised by crude conversions of war types, including the D.H.4 and D.H.9.

There were anxious times in the early days at Stag Lane, but we were all young and eager and ready to laugh at our misadventures. That gas engine, for instance, provided us with a lot of fun as well as headaches. The other directors and I always took a picnic lunch with us and when fine had it sitting on the grass with our backs to the engine house. Two engine men used to come to try to start the reluctant engine after lunch, one named Bill, who hardly ever spoke, while the other talked incessantly and cheerfully. 'Give 'er some more gas, Bill,' we would hear; then 'Give 'er some air, Bill.' Still there would be no result except a grunt. More gas and more air were given from time to time, and then: 'Now let's wind 'er up, Bill.' One day they must have pumped the whole exhaust system full of a perfect explosive mixture, and there was a shattering explosion that left us numb for the moment, and must have been heard for miles. While we were getting unsteadily to our feet ready to search for the two corpses, a voice came through, slightly surprised, but still cheerful: ' 'Ear that bloody bang, Bill?'

But more serious blows than this soon threatened to kill de Havillands even before we had got into our stride. Our first chairman was not a success. He was not our choice, his appointment being the only condition laid down by Holt Thomas who had a strange faith in him. Our chairman was interested in some other companies which seemed to be much less substantial than our own, and more than one of them failed with unenviable publicity. The next set-back was even more severe. The owners of Stag Lane from whom we rented the premises suddenly demanded that we bought it or get out, their price being £20,000. No doubt they looked on this as smart business, knowing that we had fairly firmly established ourselves and were committed to a certain amount of construction work, including eight D.H.34 airliners for Daimler Airlines and Instones. We took a pretty poor view of their business methods, and we were certainly in a fix. They demanded £7,500 'down' at once. Of course we could not meet this from our own resources, and could see no way of raising the money from outside.

One day a Mr. Alan Butler came to Stag Lane and said to St. Barbe: 'Can you design and build a private aeroplane for me, fitted with a Rolls-Royce Falcon engine?'

St. Barbe knew Butler was a rich man, but was rather staggered by such an unusual request.

'Yes, of course, we would like to, but it would cost a lot of money as a 'one off' job.'

'Well, here is a specification of what I want, and when you have got out a price, I will come and see you again.'

When St. Barbe told me of the interview I hardly took it seriously and said: 'It will probably come to nothing, so ask £3,500. It would pay us at that price, but it is sure to put him off.'

Butler came back in a few days, and when St. Barbe

gave him this figure, he replied, 'That's all right, will you please start right away. I will, of course, pay a deposit.'

We did not realize it at the time, but this was the beginning of an association with Alan Butler that was to have a vital effect on the future of our company. Shortly afterward I met Alan Butler at Stag Lane and we talked of private flying, about which we were both equally keen. He had flown a lot in England and also around the Caribbean area, and was doing his Army training when the war ended. Then one of those unlikely but fortunate events occurred that happen in novels and plays, but seldom in real life.

Quite unexpectedly, Butler said, 'Can you people do with some more capital? I'm keen to invest in an aircraft company, especially one interested in civil aeroplanes.'

Here was a heaven-sent answer to the problem which had suddenly become such a serious threat to our very existence. I explained the whole matter to him, and he said casually, as if it meant nothing at all to him, 'I'll be glad to advance £10,000, if that will help.'

Later, Butler considerably increased his investment, was elected a director of the company in 1921, and in 1924 became our chairman.

Unlike many rich men, Alan Butler, although quite young, tried to spend and invest his money wisely and was usually successful. He flew whenever possible in British as well as in European competitions, in 1928 obtained the world speed record for light two-seater machines and flew to the Cape with his clever and attractive wife, Lois, who was herself a pilot. As well as his accomplishments in the air, he was greatly interested in the sea and sailing. He held a yacht master's certificate and sailed his own yacht, *Sylvia*, four times across the Atlantic. My wife and I became close friends with Alan and Lois Butler and flew with them on many trips abroad in our Moths. Alan Butler was of medium height and dark, and gave the impression of having great reserves of nervous energy which he sometimes used with a single-minded ruthlessness that led to overwork and illness. But he also had a keen sense of humour and was a delightful companion when we went out in the evening for some fun and a show in London.

With the solution of our money problems, for the present, our work at Stag Lane steadily increased. It was varied in kind, including repair work, making various equipment for the Royal Air Force and the airlines, hiring out converted D.H.9s with pilot, starting flying training, and so on. Before we left Airco we had obtained a contract from the Air Ministry for a cantilever monoplane of wood construction to carry eight to ten passengers. We had put this forward as a logical step following the D.H.18 biplane. A prototype was constructed, and on making the first test flight I found something unusual in the control, especially in landing. At first this was a mystery, but one day when Walker and I were looking at the wind tunnel model we thought we could *see* that the wing section was different from that intended, and this proved to be so. A serious error had crept in in making the model. Our trouble then was to correct the error, do more wind tunnel tests and if all was well then to start production. But time being the main factor, we could not give the guarantee the airlines required. It was hoped that this monoplane would be supplied to the Daimler Airlines and also to Instones, but after more testing we decided that it was not ready for production and as the airlines wanted new equipment as soon as possible we decided to revert to the well-tried biplane. This decision resulted in the D.H.34, an improved version of the D.H.18, with the pilot in front of the wings instead of behind. Production was straightforward and rapid, and the aircraft performed well and was in service for some years.

We had a few orders for various military prototypes, but designing and building war machines in peacetime was very difficult. The reason for this was, briefly, that the urgency created by the war did not exist in peacetime,

116

Government officials had time to frame numbers of well-meaning but harmful regulations, the chief result of which was to slow up design and also production. There were all sorts of pet ideas which led to a never ending stream of modifications, with the result that the constructor gradually lost heart and interest and the project stagnated. There was another factor. During the war a Government department dealing with armaments has to have enough first-class men to run it, but with the returning peace and a consequent cut in staff, it is the outstanding men who go into industry, while the less experienced, less practical and less ambitious are left to nag the designer and constructor with trivial queries and demands. This was the state of affairs after the 1914 War, and we found military projects more trouble than they were worth.

One example of this frustration that happened to us at Stag Lane serves to show what I mean. We had designed and built the Hercules, a three-engined wooden biplane airliner for Imperial Airways. It was highly successful and did much flying in Africa. General Trenchard flew in it and suggested it would make an efficient bomber if the minimum but necessary modifications were made. He was obviously influenced by the fact that the Hercules was faster than the D.H.9A, the standard bomber of the Royal Air Force at that time. We got a contract to proceed with the work, but very soon the trouble started. The Government technical people saw a wonderful chance to impose 'improvements' and modifications. We thought we were going to build a Hercules adapted as a bomber, but our hopes were soon dashed. Our first shock came when we were told that the wooden Hercules was now to be all metal, and the position of the engines was to be changed. These two modifications obviously involved a complete re-design. We started on this, although our enthusiasm was already on the wane. Eventually the structure took shape in the erecting shop, but partly owing to metal

117

construction being at that time something new and about which little was known, progress was painfully slow. New 'requirements' were constantly coming in, and the engines were changed three times for improved types before the aeroplane was out of the erecting shop. The naked metal structure had been in the shop so long that it was said by a would-be humorist that it was difficult to decide which was aeroplane and which was girder structure of the shop itself.

By this time we had new civil jobs of interest and promise and the bomber became a white elephant. Interest in it had long ago died. We knew of an aircraft firm badly in need of work, and persuaded the Government contract department to hand it over to this firm for finishing. After a long time it made a short and unimpressive flight and then seemed to expire from premature old age. This was an example of the deadly effect of too much official interference in the design and construction of a project, the only result being a colossal waste of time, effort and taxpayers' money.

I believe there is only one way to get good design. The buyer should draw up the shortest possible specification with the least possible number of rigid clauses, have plenty of informal talks with the designer in whom he has confidence, and when they have arrived as near as they can to agreement, the designer must then be given a free hand. There was still another reason that put us against designing war machines in peacetime. Orders did not necessarily go to the firm with the best aeroplane, but to the firm who had less work and whose 'turn' it was for an order. A high performance biplane we had made and tested was turned down for a machine of much inferior performance, and when our figures for speed were said to be wrong, we flew the loaded machine on a closed circuit and showed an officially timed speed in excess of our previous figures and, incidentally, gained an official class record. But this made no difference!

The state of affairs after the second war was totally different. Co-operation and a far better understanding existed, and in many ways we were helped instead of being hindered. This applied especially in the case of the Comet disasters.

In the early Stag Lane days we soon turned with relief to the saner business of building civil aeroplanes that were of some use and depended on real merit to get orders. We produced the D.H.50 in 1923. It was a successful effort to produce a four-seater cabin aircraft at really low cost and upkeep. Using D.H.9 wings, tail unit, and part of the fuselage, it was powered by a Puma engine, and after the briefest of test flights was flown by Alan Cobham, the great pioneer pilot, to take part in a civil aeroplane competition at Gothenburg. Charles Walker went as passenger, together with Admiral Mark Kerr and Jim Norman. The '50' won the main contest with 999 marks out of 1,000. The '50' did well for some years and over twenty were made and used extensively in Australia and by Cobham on many of his famous world flights. He flew one in the 1924 King's Cup Race and came in first. The D.H.50 was really a highly successful civil version of the original D.H.4.

I had been thinking of an ideal 'private owner's' aeroplane for some long time, partly, or perhaps largely, because I wanted one for my own use. The available engines nearly always dictate the design of an aeroplane, and as this had to be as low in cost as possible, we chose an eighty-horsepower air-cooled Renault, or Royal Aircraft Factory engine, several of which we had bought new as surplus war stock for a price that worked out at about twenty-five shillings each. The D.H.51 biplane was designed in 1924 for one of these engines, and we sold three 51s quickly. One of these went to Mr. John Carbery in Kenya, and it is still in flying condition today. It is affectionately known as 'Miss Kenya' and probably has a record life for a 'private' aeroplane of about thirty-five years. The 51 was delightful to fly, but still rather too large and expensive for the private owner. In connection with the

119

D.H.51 there was an almost unbelievable example of official red tape and stupidity. The engine of the 51 had single ignition but dual ignition was now usual and we fitted dual to the engine and made 'Y' pieces to take two sparking plugs. We did a long test at Stag Lane that was entirely successful. The Air Ministry got to hear of this and they at once said: 'But the engine was "passed out" with single ignition, and although it is probably safer with dual ignition you cannot fly outside the three-mile limit of the aerodrome with dual ignition.' This three-mile limit rule was instituted by the Air Ministry in order that experimental aircraft could be flown at all, and if trouble developed one had a good chance of getting back the three miles to the aerodrome. We said: 'But we want to fly the 51 on cross-country flights, that was largely the reason for fitting dual ignition.' They replied: 'You will be breaking the regulations if you do, and we should have to take action. If you want to fly outside the three-mile limit you must disconnect the dual ignition and fly on single ignition. But if flying inside the three-mile limit you can use dual.'

Here was a clear case where carrying out an obsolete regulation was considered far more important than the safety of the aircraft. But this happened thirty-six years ago, at a time when there was little urgency and some officials obviously found it difficult to find important work.

At about this time there was an official light 'plane movement, and in 1923 light 'plane trials were held at Lympne, motor cycle engines being used to power the 'planes. We made the single-seater D.H.53 light monoplane fitted with a twin-cylinder Douglas motor cycle engine. I flew one of the 53s from Stag Lane to Lympne, where it performed well, but I soon realized that, although delightful to fly, this size of machine was going too far towards the miniature, for even with the engines running 'all out' they were under-powered.

But the obvious lesson was not learnt, because another

120

official competition was arranged for two-seaters with an engine not exceeding 1,100 c.c. We realized that this would lead to another under-powered and useless aeroplane and did not enter for the competition. It seemed to me that what was needed was a compromise between our too big '51' and the too-small '53'. But there was no engine of the right power for the practical light 'plane I was keen to build. So we had to create one. I suggested to Frank Halford that he should cut one of the twenty-five shilling eight-cylinder vee Renaults in half and make a four-cylinder, in-line engine using existing crankshaft, cylinders and other parts and design a new crankcase and cylinder head. He did this with his usual drive and energy, and it resulted in a robust and simple engine known as the Cirrus, giving about sixty-five horsepower without being highly stressed, and therefore was far more reliable than the over-stressed, motor cycle engines. This event was to be far more important than we realized at the time.

Here we had an engine which, although not ideal, enabled me to design a light aeroplane of the kind that had dominated my thoughts for so long, and to which I could give the intense enthusiasm that is necessary for all good work. And above all, there were very few hampering official regulations to bother about, so that I had a wonderful feeling of freedom that encouraged belief in success. I had visualized the finished aeroplane long before the design was started, and the working drawings quickly began to appear. It was an all-wood biplane with four inter-wing struts in all, instead of the more usual eight. The wings were arranged to fold back along the sides of the fuselage, safely and easily, the time for the whole operation being two minutes. The aeroplane could then be housed in a shed of normal garage size, or the tail could be attached to the rear of a car for towing. It had a plywood fuselage with very adequate cockpits for two people, the passenger being in front; dual control; and, very important, a locker behind

121

the pilot for light luggage and tool kit. The landing gear was simple and could 'take' a pretty bad landing. The petrol tank above the centre section held nineteen gallons, and an extra tank could be fitted in the front cockpit.

Although I did the main layouts and G.A. drawings, the members of the drawing office soon shared my enthusiasm so that the project became a co-operative one, with many useful ideas contributed by all of us. For example, A. E. Hagg, who was then Chief Draughtsman, thought out a clever but simple differential aileron control which moved one aileron up to a much greater angle than the other was moved down. This had the effect of depressing the high wing in the case of a 'stalled' turn instead of trying to *lift* the lower wing which only *increased* the stall of that wing. This simple but effective device was patented and used by many other aircraft firms.

As the actual construction advanced day by day, I watched it with growing interest, looking forward to the time when I could step into the cockpit and do the first test flight. A keen eye was kept on safety, from the strength of the structure to the smallest items of the controls. I had the elevator and rudder control cables and turn-buckles duplicated so that if a turn-buckle was not locked after adjustment there would be no disaster. (A fatal accident due to exactly this happening was recorded on another make of aeroplane.)

This new light aircraft was intended, above all, for the amateur, for the week-end flyer, and for instruction. Simplicity and safety were of paramount importance. For the same reason, I did not feel it was suitable or good sales policy to give it only a numeral. A name had to be found, and many ideas were put forward before my enthusiasm for natural history—which remained as strong as ever—led me to seek the solution in entymology. It suddenly struck me that the name Moth was just right. It had the right sound, was appropriate, easy to remember and might well

lead to a series of Moths, all named after British insects—
Gipsy Moth, Puss Moth, Fox Moth, Hornet Moth, Hawk
Moth, Leopard Moth.

The day arrived when the Cirrus Moth, as we called
our first Moth, was standing on the aerodrome with its
dark blue fuselage and light cream wings. The registration
letters were G-EBKT. The first test flight of a new aeroplane was always for me a mixture of concentrated
interest, some excitement and a little apprehension; but
the intense interest always overcame the thought of any
danger. Testing all aeroplanes in the earlier days had much
in common and was straightforward, in comparison with
much more complex aeroplanes of today. A series of
taxiing trials were usually done first to test control on the
ground, functioning of the landing gear on rough ground
and, perhaps most important of all, the tail skid behaviour.
It is a strange fact that for many years on our new aeroplanes, tail skids collapsed in a monotonously regular way
until we made them about four times as strong as seemed
reasonable. There is no easy way of 'stressing' a tail skid.

My thoughts before opening the throttle for a first
flight were about the tail 'setting'. There were few wind
tunnel tests to go by and the tail setting was usually a
matter of a close guess. But if set at too great an angle it
might result in the pilot not being able to hold the nose up,
and if at too negative an angle, in not being able to hold it
down. Once in the air I always felt much happier and could
test elevator, aileron rudder controls and engine revs. at
leisure. The first flight was always short, because it
usually showed the need for small adjustments. Then I
carried out a more extended flight intended to test stall
performance, which was critically important in testing for
'wing drop', then climbing to a good height to test spinning and recovery. Periodically I would fly straight and
level for a few seconds to make notes on a knee pad.
Finally I ended up with a long, full throttle high speed run.

In testing the first Cirrus Moth, this same pattern was followed, and yet there was a difference. This difference was, I believe, to be found in the complete confidence I felt that this was going to be not just a good aeroplane, but that the Cirrus Moth was going to lead to a new period of simpler and easier flying for the masses. After five minutes in the air I knew my hopes were justified. We had produced something outstanding in light aeroplanes.

The Moth was one of our most successful civil designs and marked the beginning of a new era of small and medium-sized civil aircraft. At first it was looked upon as just another light 'plane, but when its qualities and performance became known it made a remarkable impact on the aviation world, and especially on light 'plane enthusiasts.

The success of the Moth was due very much to its being just the right size and of the simplest possible construction with sufficient reliable power to carry two people and some luggage. It had good cruising speed and range, low landing speed, was easy to handle and could be housed in a small shed by folding the wings. It was low in first cost and upkeep. The cruising speed was about seventy miles per hour, the range approximately three hundred miles, landing speed forty miles per hour. The first cost was £650 and we had good hopes of eventually reducing this. Owing to its sturdy and simple construction the maintenance was remarkably low.

We soon started on a small production batch of Moths and these quickly created a demand for more. Flying clubs were started at home and overseas, and production had to be speeded up to satisfy the increasing demand. Soon they were being flown by both men and women to India, Africa and Australia and most other countries. They were fitted with floats and used on water, and with skis for use on snow.

In 1926 we decided to design our own engine for the Moth, new in every item, and the one-hundred-horsepower Gipsy I was the result, this being followed by the Gipsy

Major, a very reliable engine giving 130 h.p. and used in a great number of different 'planes. This was the beginning of our own Engine Division and was done in the first place because it was too risky to rely entirely on engine supply from an outside source for our growing production of Moths. It was also the first of a long line of engines leading eventually to the modern jet turbines. The Royal Air Force became interested in the Moth as a preliminary trainer. A few minor modifications were made and the Tiger Moth was produced. This became the standard Royal Air Force trainer for many years, and is still flying in many parts of the world today, using the Gipsy Major engine.

The aeroplane has not yet developed to the stage where it can be used like a car, but Moth owners came near to it in the practical use of their 'planes. It was quite usual to fly to a place one wished to visit and land in the nearest suitable field, tether the plane down with screw pickets, then go to get permission from the farmer to land in his field. And there was seldom any trouble.

On one occasion Alan Butler and his friend, Nigel Norman, had booked seats to see a big prize fight in Paris, but they were prevented from going by sea and rail due to gale force winds and extremely heavy seas which kept ships in port and airliners grounded. Alan decided to fly over in his Gipsy Moth with Norman as passenger. With people hanging on to the wings and tail to prevent it being blown over during taxiing, Alan gave the order to 'let go' and was in the air in a few yards. They arrived safely after a rough passage, and were said to be the only visitors from England to arrive in Paris on that day.

With the Moth, in all its guises and derivatives, we had not only started a new era of cheap and convenient flying; we had built ourselves security and the foundations on which the large de Havilland enterprise of today was erected. By the mid 1920s we were no longer anxious enthusiasts struggling for recognition; we had arrived.

CHAPTER EIGHT

FAMILY LIFE AND FLYING

WHEN our two eldest boys, Geoffrey and Peter, were six and three years old, I thought it was time that they were introduced seriously to flying, so I took them up in a very docile and slow-landing D.H.6 trainer from Hendon. They were only mildly excited at the prospect of this event, and when I got them into the air they remained totally unimpressed. Peter took no notice at all, except to spit over the side 'to see where it would go', and would have been more excited by a motor-car journey; while Geoffrey, whose passion at the time was for trains, kept his eye on the railway line to see where it went. For them, and for their younger brother, John, the flying urge came later; in their early years their interests ranged from traction engines to sports cars, from trams to natural history. John was the great naturalist, and all through his boyhood we shared an enthusiasm for country life, and he became an expert at the identification of birds and insects and wild animals, and learnt to ride, shoot and fish well.

Louie and I had once hired a horse caravan for a great butterflying trip in the New Forest in order to get away from the hurly-burly of Stag Lane. Shortly after this I built on aircraft construction principles and to my own design a trailer caravan, using spruce members with three-ply covering. At week-ends and for holidays we would tow this behind the car to the edge of a large wood I knew from my boyhood and where I had 'collected' off and on for twenty-five years. The site was ideally remote and I used to love the silence there as dusk approached, soon to be broken by the call of plovers and curlews, the almost continuous 'churring' of the nightjars and the hum of the insects. It was all wonderfully soothing after the noise and anxieties at Stag Lane, and as the years went by I found ever greater pleasure in the beauties and delights of that remote corner of Hampshire, but the caravan was too small for us all and so we built a cottage not far from our old rectory at Crux Easton. We still have this cottage and go down occasionally for long week-ends. It has been tended and kept spick and span for many years by my first wife's sister, Lottie Thomas. When John was young he always wanted to live there, and spent most of his holidays at the cottage. When he died it was a numbing blow for poor Lottie who had loved John deeply ever since he was a baby.

Peter's great interest in life was sport, and he later played cricket for Stowe in the public schools match at Lord's. Today he works on the sales side of the company, is happily married to a very attractive wife, Joy, and has two children of his own, Peter Geoffrey and Anne.

But of course it was the aeroplane that remained the dominant theme in the lives of all of us—and I would not have had it otherwise. The boys had been brought up within the almost continuous sound of aircraft on the ground or in the air, and when they went on from prep school to Stowe, Louie and I would always visit them by Moth, landing in a field within the school grounds and there eating our picnic lunches. Neither Geoffrey nor Peter was brilliant at work, but Geoffrey was a good long distance runner and Peter a keen cricketer; then, after a short period abroad to have some of the corners rubbed off, they went through the de Havilland Technical School and learnt to fly at the London Aeroplane Club. John also learnt to fly early, and soon joined Geoffrey on test flying at Hatfield.

Flying became such an integral part of all our lives, that

127

it seemed the most natural thing in the world to select the site for our cottage alongside a largish field. For fifteen years we used our aeroplanes—Gipsy Moths followed by Puss and Leopard Moths—as a regular means of transport from Stag Lane or Hatfield to Crux Easton, folding the wings after landing and making all secure against wind and storm, for the week-end or longer. The journey by car took two hours and a quarter, by Moth less than half an hour.

At first our arrival by air at week-ends caused something of a sensation, but after a while the locals became quite accustomed to having an airborne family in their midst. A few of the more daring among the villagers sometimes asked for flights, and when they returned unharmed there was soon a rush from both young and old. Amongst my passengers were three who had the unique distinction of having flown before they had travelled in a train. An old lady of eighty-odd who had had twenty-two children arrived one day for her flight in her black beaded Sunday dress, umbrella in hand, and with her false teeth in place. (Normally she wore them only on Sundays.) She seemed mildly pleased with her flight, and certainly showed no signs of nervousness. Most of the boys and girls of the village were given flights too, and there were, naturally, many requests from time to time for jobs at our factory. I always pointed out that if they got a job it was entirely up to them to keep it, and there would be no 'influence' or favouritism, and that leaving an isolated country village for the outskirts of London might be a rather unpleasant shock. But of those who took the plunge, not one let me down, and most of them did really well and are in good positions today, some having been with us for twenty or twenty-five years. The boys were typical country lads, most of them being farm workers. One of those who applied and did very well was a gamekeeper's son who had not long left the village school, had never been in a

128

train and only a few times to the country town seven miles away. When I asked him later if he had been home-sick, he admitted that at first it was sheer misery and he thought constantly of the great wood at Crux Easton where he used to search for pheasants' nests and take some of the eggs for hatching under hens in coops, often going all day without seeing another living soul. Stag Lane with its crowded workshops and constant din of machinery must have seemed a hellish place at first, but it is obvious that for some people the attraction of the cities and the desire to become one of the crowd with the chance of earning more money often provide more than all that the country-side can offer.

Through all the years between the wars, and in spite of my growing responsibilities and the time my desk de-manded of me, I continued to fly all our 'planes whenever opportunity occurred, and put in many hundreds of flying hours. The sheer pleasure of flying, combined with the technical fascination of testing, never lost their appeal. I even did a certain amount of competition flying, for fun as well as for the prestige victory would give the Company. With the advent of the more powerful Gipsy Moth, I entered each year for the King's Cup Air Race. One year Geoffrey joined me as passenger, and by a piece of mis-judgement I came near to killing us both. The course from London included Glasgow as a turning point and then went south over the mountains of Cumberland. We were flying above cloud at the time, but did catch one glimpse of the sea coast on our right, which led me to believe that we had left the high ground behind. So I put the nose down and lost height through the thick cloud, expecting to emerge at least a thousand feet above the ground. After quite a short descent I was mystified to see strange greyish-white lumps in front of us. It took me, I suppose, less than a tenth of a second to react to this sudden danger; but even that was almost too long. With the stick pulled back hard towards me, the undercarriage just missed by a few feet the grazing sheep on the rock-strewn summit of a mountain.

The King's Cup could usually be depended on to provide some excitement. On another occasion and in a Puss Moth with one of our design team as passenger, we were over Yorkshire when I thought I noticed a faint smell of burning. At once the engine began to race wildly, and I pulled back the throttle. I was rather surprised to find we no longer had a propeller. It had flown off the engine, luckily in one piece, and there had been scarcely a jar as it left the machine. (If a propeller breaks and only one blade comes off, the out-of-balance forces are so great that the whole engine is usually torn from the aeroplane in a fraction of a second.) We were not high at the time, and it was necessary to decide pretty quickly on a field in which to land. It had all happened so suddenly and this, coupled with the fact that instead of the steady roar of the engine there was now silence, may have caused me some momentary bewilderment. Not that this mattered for there was no choice—it had to be a field of growing corn. The landing was what is known as 'heavy', in other words bad, and the undercarriage collapsed. A farm worker brought us the propeller almost undamaged. We traced the trouble later and found it was one of those rare cases of error in fitting the propeller to the hub on the engine shaft.

Flying in the King's Cup Air Race was good sport, but after a few years of it I gave up all hope of winning and was content to share in the general excitement and derive satisfaction and interest from following a set course round England. Plenty of skill and care were demanded for usually the visibility was poor over some of the course, and you had sometimes to fly high and sometimes low so as to take advantage of wind direction. The throttle remained fully open from start to finish. But in 1933 we had our new Leopard Moth, a three-seater, and a much improved version of the Puss Moth. I flew the first one we built in the 1933 King's Cup Air Race, and had a great and pleasant surprise when I was able to come in first and win the Cup with a speed of 140 miles an hour. I owned this Leopard Moth until the outbreak of the 1939 War when all light aircraft were taken over by the Government. This marked the end of a great era of private ownership and private flying in Britain. In those happy flying years there were few tiresome regulations, everything was simple, and even the first and running costs were not unreasonable. After the last war there was almost no market for new light aeroplanes, they cost three or four times as much to build, and very few would-be owners could afford any sort of 'plane.

*

It was a blessing that Louie enjoyed flying almost as much as I did, and as soon as I recognized how enthusiastic she was we flew everywhere together, all over England, the Continent and Africa. These trips were by no means frivolous joyriding; each had a definite purpose and served as a most useful prolonged test, of new components or of the 'plane itself. We loved going off at short notice to places on the Continent, one of our longest trips being to Berlin. Alan Butler and his wife, Lois, went with us in their own Moth. While there we met the German pilot, Udet, who at that time was doing exhibition stunt flying in his own biplane. He was most interested in the Moth, and we had a friendly competition at Tempelhof Airport, when I was able to demonstrate the Gipsy Moth. Udet was a rather tough type with very limited technical knowledge, in fact smallish both physically and mentally. But he was very popular with the German people as a daring stunt pilot. He was given a high position in the German Air Force when war broke out, and having met him many times I could hardly imagine a less suitable man for the high position he held. As the war intensified so did Udet's responsibilities, possibly to save Goering from the verdict of failure. The burden was too great for Udet. He took to drink in a big way and shot himself before the end of the war.

Our trip to Berlin had given Louie and me ideas for a longer flight; and when I suggested a visit to North Africa in 1929 she readily agreed. Africa always was, and still is, for me the most fascinating of all places, and although we had seen a little of the north coast and Cairo during a trip in 1927, it only made us want to go again to see more. We intended to go via Paris, through France, over the Pyrenees, through Spain and Morocco, in our open cockpit Gipsy Moth. I had an additional five-gallon tank fixed in the front cockpit and fitted a slightly larger windscreen for the pilot's cockpit. Thus equipped, and with the minimum of baggage, we set off on one of the most fascinating journeys in my life. It is hard to describe the pleasure, satisfaction and sense of independence to be found in flying a light 'plane over the Continent in fine weather, dropping in for a meal or a night's sleep at almost any town or village that takes your fancy. As well, of course, there were more unpleasant and more anxious occasions on that trip. When fog defeated us across a part of France, we were forced to follow the coastline of Spain to avoid the more mountainous regions, and finally landed unannounced at Barcelona, which was a military aerodrome in a state of some tension due to current political trouble. I nearly lost my precious new stereoscopic camera there—and the Moth and both our lives on the way back home from North Africa later. This unpleasantness occurred over Spain between Burgos and Biarritz, after being recommended by the Spanish Air Force that the only practical way was over the western Pyrenees. I tried for some time to follow narrow valleys between vertical walls of rock, feeling horribly vulnerable and insignificant, but we were managing well enough until one particularly nasty valley closed right in on us.

A quick decision had to be made, whether to fly over the rock wall on our left, or turn round the narrowing gorge and go back. It was then that I thought of a small bottle of liquid which a friend had given me at Gibraltar, saying that it might be useful. It had remained unsampled and was still in the cockpit. I took a swallow, and the result was almost instantaneous and quite remarkable. When I could see again, and looked at the summit of the rock wall it looked far less menacing, and, putting the Moth to maximum climb at full throttle, we crept over the edge, dodging the broken clouds. I was interested to know more about this strange drink, and when next I saw our friend she told me she could not remember the exact proportions, but when mixing it she started with whisky, added some brandy, a portion of gin, and some sherry 'to give it flavour', but no water. I had never before taken alcohol when flying, but found one small drink of this mixture did help in restoring confidence when in a difficult situation. But it would be very easy to overdo it and then be in real trouble. Alcohol is best left severely alone when piloting an aircraft.

After the cold and the buffeting we endured on that trip I was more keen than ever to design a light cabin aeroplane which would do away with the draughts and discomforts of open cockpit flying. The Puss Moth was the result. With this machine there was none of the tiring rush of air, no necessity for goggles and caps, bulky leather flying clothing and clumsy speaking tubes; the cabin was heated, there was plenty of luggage space, all the comforts of a saloon car, and a higher performance and longer range than the earlier Moth, due to the better aerodynamic form. The Puss Moth was a high-wing, strut-braced monoplane with room for pilot and two passengers, and wings that could still be folded. We also 'inverted' the engine, which gave better forward visibility, did away with the curse of oil spray on the windscreen and provided less air resistance.

When I took the Puss Moth up for its first flight in September 1929 I discovered that it came right up to expectation. It was extremely comfortable and could take three people twenty miles on a gallon of petrol at 100 m.p.h., a performance that no motor-car has ever achieved. At Crux Easton, however, on my first flight down to the cottage, I found great difficulty in getting into the field, because the gliding angle of the 'plane was about the same as the field's gradient. The landing gear struts were long, telescopic streamlined tubes containing rubber blocks. These tubes were later made to rotate through ninety degrees so that they could be turned broadside to the air and thus form an efficient air brake. That solved the landing problem admirably.

It was the Puss Moth that first took me to South Africa in 1932. Charles Walker and I had to go out there and back to investigate two accidents to this 'plane, travelling by ship, railway, motor-car, and our own Hercules airliner—the largest we had built and just starting to fly the African route—and Nile steamer to Cairo. By then I had seen enough of the real Africa to want to visit the continent again in more leisurely style, and three years later I was able to get away with Louie for three months' holiday in Kenya. We both fell in love with the place, with its vastness that gives a new concept of space and distance, and the solitude which I have always sought for the peace and tranquillizing effect it has on me.

Since those days I have made perhaps a dozen trips to East Africa, and each has added new and memorable experiences. I have followed the valley of the White Nile in one of our own Rapide aircraft, been on many safaris in Kenya, Uganda and Tanganyika and innumerable natural history expeditions in search of new examples to photograph and add to my collection. I even went big-game hunting with a rifle, but found this so completely distasteful that I never tried again, taking up with much greater enthusiasm the photography of wild game.

Even today, when I feel that wonderful part of the world, with its great panoramas, colour and excitement drawing me back, I usually manage to find the excuse to travel out again, visiting some of the many friends I have made there over the years. Two friends we never fail to see are Eric and Bettie Walker who built the hotel in Nyeri where we always stay. They also found, many years ago, an ideal site in a forest only ten miles away where a host of wild animals could be observed from a 'house' built in a Giant Fig tree and now world-renowned as 'Tree Tops'. Eric Walker and I had met in France in the First World War when we were both in the R.F.C. and it was quite by chance that we met again after seventeen years, in Kenya. Eric has always been a close and real friend and we hope to visit Nyeri and to see Eric and Bettie many more times.

CHAPTER NINE

THE RECORD BREAKERS

EVERY new means of transport since the industrial revolution has had its romantic period, this usually occurring between the first experimental days and the time when it becomes accepted by the masses and develops into big business. For the steam locomotive this took place in the 1830s and 1840s, the pioneering period for the motor-car was the Edwardian era, for the aeroplane it followed the First World War.

Flying and the aeroplane were still at the experimental and tentative stage in the early 1920s, even though they were accepted as commonplace within a strictly limited orbit. Range was still restricted to a few hundred miles, and regular passenger travel across the Atlantic seemed as far away as a rocket service to the moon appears to us today. Above all, flying was still regarded with some awe and as a highly specialized skill beyond the ability of the average man or woman.

It was with the idea of dispelling this belief, of bringing flying out of the rarefied field of activity, and of popularizing light 'plane flying with our own Moth—which was so eminently suitable for the purpose—that we started the London Aeroplane Club at Stag Lane. I believe it was Frank Hearle's idea originally, backed by The Royal Aero Club, and a very shrewd one it was. For many years it was accepted as one of the most suitable places at which to learn to fly, and, after qualification, to use as a base and to keep your aircraft. All the machines used were D.H. Moths, in one form or another.

Many people who were to become famous in the world of aviation began their flying career at Stag Lane, and the most pleasing and romantic aspect of the school was the unexpectedly large number of women who came to learn to fly, of whom many were to become popular heroines through their record-breaking activities. I think it is true to say that in flying, for which the Moth provided the means, the Englishwoman's new-found emancipation found its freest form of expression. Not that all of them, by any means, were young. Among those whom I knew well, and for whom I had the highest regard, was Lady Bailey who was thirty-five when in July 1927 she took off in a Gipsy Moth with Louie and climbed to 17,289 feet, a height record for a woman flying a light 'plane at that time. Lady Bailey, a daughter of the fifth Lord Rossmore and the wife of Sir Abe Bailey the South African industrialist, was the mother of five children, but did not allow this to interfere in any way with the flying activities which she loved. After qualifying in a Moth at Stag Lane in 1926, she became the first woman to fly the Irish Sea, and with her spectacular flight to South Africa in 1928 helped Amy Johnson to blaze the trail of solo flights all over the world that became so fashionable later. On one of her flights to the Cape I saw her off from Stag Lane on a misty day when the aerodrome was almost waterlogged. When she opened the throttle of her heavily-loaded Puss Moth it was scarcely able to move, and I had to put my shoulder to it before she could gather way. Her take-off run seemed to occupy the full length of the aerodrome, but at last she wallowed off into the mist in her tiny machine. It seemed highly unlikely that she would ever make the coast, but she turned up all right in North Africa, after a non-stop flight, where she promptly developed influenza and wasted a day! She made great numbers of long flights all over the

137

world, nearly always alone and much of the time flying 'blind' in darkness or mist and cloud. She had an almost off-hand attitude towards flying, talking about it in the simplest and most amateur manner. But this was deceptive, for she knew much more about the technique of navigation under almost impossible conditions than most people were prepared to credit. I cannot recollect her having a flying accident, but she did have one unusual mishap that might have been fatal. She started her engine one day at Stag Lane by swinging the propeller in the usual way and slipped forward on the wet grass. The result of this sort of miscalculation was often fatal, but Lady Bailey was only scalped. I happened to be there at the time and retrieved the large patch of skin and hair from the ground; and I believe it was later cleaned and bound into place. When I next saw her two or three weeks later she was wearing a sort of turban; but this did not prevent her from flying.

Another more elderly lady pilot who flew our Moths, but, as befitted her rank, learnt to fly privately in the grounds of her ancestral home, was the Duchess of Bedford. This remarkable woman was no temporary or fair weather pilot, but gave to flying the enthusiasm she devoted to all her activities so that she was soon both capable and reliable. While she was still being instructed she suffered the disappointment of being prevented from taking a certain test by her instructor because of bad weather. She took him to the cinema instead. It happened that a film of mine of the life history of the swallowtail butterfly, which I had made as a pastime but which had been bought by a film company, was being shown at the local cinema. A few days later I received a letter from her saying that her disappointment at not being able to take her test had been quite forgotten in the pleasure she had experienced in seeing this film. This was typical of the courtesy and thoughtfulness of this very kind woman. Many people will remember that the Duchess of Bedford died flying, the activity she loved best in the world. She just flew over the East Coast in her Moth in bad weather and was never seen again. I was interested to see in the recent autobiography of the present Duke, that he strongly suspects what I had long believed: that her death was no accident. It seems that her husband had recently told her that he could no longer support her other great interest, the private hospital she had run so efficiently during the war. This, I know, was a great blow; but worse was to come when she learnt unofficially that, because of her age, the authorities would not renew her flying licence.

A spectacular pair to earn their wings at Stag Lane were Pauline Gower and Dorothy Spicer, who showed great enterprise during the period when flying circuses were all the rage by setting up on their own. For some years they toured the country, giving 'joy' rides for a small fee. For a time they were with Cobham's 'Circus', and when war threatened they turned their talent to more serious purpose, Pauline Gower becoming a Commissioner of the Civil Air Guard and later Commandant of the women's section of the Air Transport Auxiliary. She died tragically in 1947 giving birth to twin sons.

The A.T.A. benefited greatly from the flying skill of these young girls acquired at Stag Lane, and later at Hatfield when the London Aeroplane Club moved there. I shall never forget the surprise I got the first time I saw a slim girl in blue slacks climbing out of the cockpit of a great Lancaster bomber, strolling over to the watch tower as if she had been delivering 'planes all her life. Lois Butler, the wife of our chairman, was one of the most skilled of the A.T.A. girls; although 'girls' is hardly the right word, for Lois was a grandmother when she delivered her eighty-second Mosquito, a high-powered and pretty heavily loaded warplane.

But the most celebrated pair in the A.T.A., as they had been as a result of their record-breaking flights before the

war, were Amy Johnson and Jim Mollison. Amy was certainly the most successful of all the young girls who earned
their wings at Stag Lane, and she received enough adula-
tion from the British public to tax the nerves and modesty
of any woman. Her first great success after leaving the
Yorkshire solicitor's office in which she had been working
was her flight to Darwin in Australia in a Gipsy Moth in
nineteen and a half days—a ridiculously long time by today's standards but unprecedented at that time. When 'our
Amy' returned to Croydon there were two hundred thousand waiting to greet her. 'Publicity would in time drive
me insane,' she wrote to me at this time in answer to my
letter of congratulation, 'and I am therefore taking the
cowardly action of running away from it . . . I feel that the
unwanted and overdone publicity I have received has just
about ruined any aviation career I might have had in this
country . . . My one desire is to be left in peace to fly.'
But that was not to be. Her later exploits included flights
of six days to India, four days to Cape Town, and the
first woman's solo flight across the Atlantic. When she
married Jim Mollison in 1933 she must somehow have
rationalized her attitude to publicity, for in those drab days
of unemployment and anxiety the pair represented in the
British mind the glittering ideal of youthful romance and
courage that even Hollywood could not match. During the
war she was delivering a 'plane from the north of England and came down in the Thames Estuary in very bad
weather. She was seen in the freezing, rough seas by the
crew of a warship, and a Lieutenant-Commander Fletcher
dived in in an attempt to save her; but both died. I always
liked Amy and we got on well together. She always used
to come to see me to discuss her plans before setting off on
a flight, bringing along her charts and itinerary. I never
ceased to admire the thoroughness and care with which
she prepared her expeditions, and of course, her courage
and skill in the air became a by-word.

The Record Breakers

There were many others, equally colourful and almost as successful as Amy, like Winifred Spooner, Beryl Markham and Jean Batten. 'Try Again Jean' or 'Third-Time-Lucky Jean'—how the Press loved these soubriquets—was the youngest and surely the smallest and most game of the London Aeroplane Club girls. It was Squadron Leader Bert Hinkler's Australia–Britain air record in 1928 that inspired her, she once told me, and soon after this she persuaded her parents to allow her to leave New Zealand to complete her musical training in London. The piano she had been given was soon sold to pay for flying lessons instead, and after she qualified she contrived by goodness knows what methods to acquire the finance for her record flights, Lord Wakefield being among her promoters. She had a great many crashes and ill luck—in spite of the black cat she carried everywhere as a mascot—but in due course beat most of Amy's records, with a South Atlantic flight—the first woman to cross that ocean—in thirteen hours, England to Brazil in two and a half days, and England to Australia in five days, twenty-one hours, among many other achievements.

*

Even before most of these young women learnt to fly at Stag Lane, the craze for record-breaking long distance flights had set in. In the course of time this record-breaking business became something of a farce, as well as highly dangerous. One pilot, for example, who claimed a record flight explained to me that it was 'because it was the first time a pilot had taken his own wife on a long flight instead of someone else's.' I knew an airline pilot—he was the pilot of the Hercules, our first large airliner, in which my wife and I flew to Cairo in 1927—who planned to fly the Atlantic with a well-known lady passenger. He asked me over to Brooklands to see his aircraft, a single-engined American monoplane, a good machine, but the project seemed to me as hazardous as most of the other Atlantic attempts. Anti-icing devices had not yet been developed, and he had chosen a most unsuitable time of the year when icing conditions were prevalent. 'Don't you think this is a very risky job?' I asked him, since he had asked my advice. But he brushed this aside. 'I have considered every possible hazard and have done very thorough fuel consumption tests. I've left nothing to chance—nothing can stop me.' Shortly after this they started from the west of England in poor weather and were never heard of again.

Cobham would never have considered anything so foolhardy. Alan Cobham—now knighted of course—was at one time on our staff, and became a brilliant pilot who made a great number of successful long distance flights to all parts of the world. He had tremendous energy and stamina —two assets in that game. I remember him rushing in for lunch one day (he nearly always ran everywhere) saying he had to be off on a flight in ten minutes. He began at once, and I watched in fascination as, talking constantly, he put whole potatoes and chunks of meat and bread in his mouth as if he were stoking a furnace instead of eating. He was still swallowing and still talking as he raced for the aerodrome, leapt into his aircraft and tore off—forever chasing time. He never seemed to suffer indigestion, either! After his successful record-breaking flying career, he started to develop an idea born during his long flights: refuelling in the air. At first he could get no response, but by great perseverance and hard work over many years he eventually won recognition and formed Flight Refuelling Ltd., which is today a flourishing concern. I have always been very fond of Alan and find him a constant stimulation. He is blessed with the energy of ten men, and works like twenty; a sight always refreshing to witness.

A very different young man came to us at Stag Lane in the early days. He was still at Oxford and applied to us to

be allowed to work on aeronautics during the long vaca-
tion. We agreed, and this quiet and studious student
arrived at Stag Lane. He was clearly an able mathematician and possessed a good knowledge of aerodynamics,
which was a surprising acquisition in those days. When
Nevil Shute Norway came down we took him on per-
manently and he did a lot of good work for us before
leaving to take on a high technical position in the building
of the Vickers airship, R100. With Hessell Tiltman, another ex-member of our staff, he formed the Airspeed
Company, which was for a time highly successful. But the
urge to write had been nagging at him all through these
years, and as he became more famous as a novelist, he
gradually dropped out of aviation. Skilled as he was, I
doubt whether he could have attained in aeronautics the
fame he acquired as a novelist, a fame which was enhanced
in an unusual way when his knowledge of aeronautics
appeared in a strangely prophetic way in *No Highway*.
Many people at the time thought that in this novel he forecast in a most dramatic way the fatigue trouble that led to
the Comet disasters. There was some truth in this, but it
did not bear too close examination. Norway had always
been a keen student of 'flutter', and quite correctly forecast
that a new and much faster airliner might bring with it (as
it had often done in the past) new problems of flutter which
could lead to metal fatigue. It was, of course, the effect of
pressurized cabins on metal fatigue that caused the Comet 1
failure, but Norway's point was well made nevertheless
and gave his readers as well a very good story.

CHAPTER TEN

DESIGN AND PROGRESS

IT HAS always seemed to me that the people carrying out the work of administration and finance have the hardest, most uninteresting and thankless jobs. I suppose I hold this view because I had no ability nor liking for these essential branches of the de Havilland Company and therefore looked on them with awe and bewilderment; but I have always had the highest regard for those who deal so efficiently with these complex matters. When, as occasionally happens, a very successful aircraft is produced, it is the designer who comes in for most of the publicity and praise, but he could have achieved nothing without the toil and hard work of those in offices and workshops. From the beginning, Hearle, Nixon and St. Barbe and their staffs carried out the administration, finance and general business of the firm, while I dreamed about new designs with a sort of one-track mind. I found it impossible to escape from these obsessional thoughts of design and flying. When I started on my first aeroplane the desire to do everything was almost fanatical, and I felt an almost fierce resentment against outside help. Perhaps this was an unconscious desire to prove that it could be done alone—I do not know. I do know that the design and production of good aeroplanes has always been to me infinitely more important and rewarding than just making money.

But there inevitably came a time when the desire to do everything in design had to give way to reasonable co-operation with others. The days of the one-man show were over. Having done a layout of a new type it was discussed with the chief designer and the aerodynamics people; and design thereby at once became a combined effort. As aircraft became larger and more complex, more specialized departments were required. Wind tunnels for high speeds, computers and an increased static testing programme became necessary. Today the design of a modern aeroplane is an immense and costly undertaking, very far removed from the primitive hit-or-miss methods of my first efforts. But mathematicians, computers and wind tunnels, although very necessary, cannot design a successful aeroplane; today the creative brain of the designer is just as essential as it has always been.

Although most designers would resent being called an artist and respond that they could not draw well nor paint at all, a designer must have much of the creative artist in him, backed up by a lot of practical engineering experience. A successful designer is born rather than made, and is a rare product. Neither a deep knowledge of mathematics nor great theoretical knowledge is necessary. In the case of an aircraft designer he will have a stress department to call on for strength calculations and an aerodynamics department to call on for data on performance, control, stability, areas and sections of surfaces, etc. It is not easy to analyse the mental process of designing; primarily it is previous experience and thought concentration, and I think most designers have the gift for creating a mental picture and visualizing shape, size, relationship between parts, and thus build up a basic image which can later be transferred to the drawing board where it will go through many changes before finality. A deep insight into mechanical engineering is one of the chief essentials, and that is why practical experience, and lots of it, is so essential. Not only has each detail part to be strong enough, but it must be as easy as possible to make, to repair, to maintain and to replace. These features have little to do with the theoretical aspect, they are more matters of experience and common sense.

To be successful a designer must have the enthusiasm and assured self-confidence that will enable him to take full responsibility for a great project that may involve millions of pounds. He will be supported by a team of his own choosing, but after careful consideration of suggestions that may be put forward by his staff, vital decisions remain his alone. He must have the strength of will to refuse to take on more work than can be done efficiently and well, however strongly he is pressed to do so by the uninitiated. He will infuse his team with his own enthusiasm and high standards of work, and this can be a precious legacy that will live on indefinitely after him. I could point to several famous firms where the high ideal born many years ago is still actively alive today. Anything well designed is a work of art, and many people get as much pleasure and inspiration from a finely designed machine or structure as others get from fine pictures or sculpture.

The Gipsy Moth was one of our very successful designs, but there were some other designs which could be classed as failures, and it is interesting to analyse why there were these failures. In most cases it became clear that the man put in charge of the design was unsuitable, and the chief designer had not sufficient time to supervise the design continuously. In other words, we were trying to do too much at one time, and this resulted in aircraft that usually failed through being overweight. In one case I was persuaded against my better judgement to get out drawings for a side-by-side two-seater with extra slow landing features. The sales people were very keen about it and were sure that it would sell well, but I was never really convinced. The wide cabin for two side-by-side seats did not make for speed. It was built, and a fair number were sold, but it could not compete with the other cabin Moths. The lesson to be learnt from this case was that it is a mistake to try to give a prospective buyer all that he asks for. He will often ask for the impossible and is disappointed when he doesn't get it.

Two designs were 'killed' by allowing buyers to modify the specification during construction of the aircraft. They demanded more range and payload than originally specified, and instead of our refusing to alter the design we unwisely tried to modify, and this led to an unsatisfactory compromise. The buyers were, of course, perfectly justified in asking for what they wanted, but should have been told that it would mean re-design and much delay.

These two cases accentuate the vital importance of working to a carefully thought out specification which must, in no case, be seriously modified at a later date. If necessary, the design should be scrapped and started anew. The design of an aircraft is governed primarily by the power of the engine, and this power cannot suddenly be increased, and there is seldom a quite suitable alternative engine available. If a design is significantly modified during construction it is almost bound to lead to failure and great loss in money and goodwill.

This also raises the point about the difference between draughtsmen and designers. A man may be an excellent draughtsman but useless as a designer. He may be extremely good at managing a drawing office, have a good knowledge of mathematics and aerodynamics, and yet produce an aircraft fit only for immediate burning. I have known several of this type, and each was a square peg in a round hole. Some years ago our Technical School students were invited to submit individual design studies for a light 'plane, and from time to time I was asked to look them over. I found that it was nearly always possible to spot the outstanding design. On one occasion I realized that one design was a long way ahead of all the others, although there were several much above the average.

It is not easy to explain why I realized this difference.

In the case in question I was impressed by the 'form' and efficiency of the design, every part had obviously been thought out and all fell into place to form a harmonious whole.

The student, Philip Smith, who was responsible for this design, is now holding a very high position in our design office, and is in charge of one of the most important of our new projects, the D.H.121, or Trident Airliner.

There are many useful people who can turn their hand to anything. They are certainly as important, if not more important, than the specialist. But by definition alone, the specialist must specialize in his own field to the exclusion of all others, doing the work that, in many cases, comes near to being an obsession. I believe this applies to design work especially, whether for aircraft or anything else; although there are of course the privileged few who are good at almost anything to which they turn their hands.

There are many first-class aircraft designers who do not fly themselves. They are almost certainly better equipped with aerodynamic knowledge than I was when I started, and therefore the knowledge I gained by doing a lot of flying is less necessary to them, but I still think that flying helps a designer very considerably, as long as he really enjoys it.

I have mentioned earlier that we found the designing of aircraft in peacetime was very difficult. After the 1914–18 War it became clear that the demands of civil and military aviation would tend to diverge in important respects. Commercial aircraft would require the best performance attainable for the power used in order to become paying propositions, and this meant the lowest possible first cost and maintenance cost. In military aircraft, performance was the first requirement at almost any cost, and economical running costs were hardly considered. These conditions led to aeroplanes for civil use developing all possible increase of 'cleanness' and efficiency; and as speed increased and fixed propellers were designed to deal with it, these propellers became very unsuitable for starting from rest and taking off. The need for variable pitch propellers (which can be likened to a motor-car's gearbox) became really urgent when little more than half the engine power was converted into thrust as compared with eighty per cent at speed.

The rules for certifying engines included the limiting of engine revolutions on climb and in full out flying. In time these rules were looked upon almost as laws of nature which could not be transgressed. New rules were required regarding engine revolutions that would allow the use of variable pitch propellers. This was done in America after 1918. Charles Walker had written an article drawing attention to the great importance of variable pitch propellers in enabling greater performance to be obtained without increasing the power, and we tried to arouse Air Ministry interest in this country—quite without success. The Hele-Shaw variable pitch propeller was being developed with government help, but so slowly that it seemed to be years away from production and general use. So we arranged to take out a licence for the American Hamilton Standard variable pitch propeller because it was the most developed. But it required the Battle of Britain, with the Hurricanes and Spitfires at a critical time adding greatly to their ceiling and speed, to show how essential was a variable pitch propeller, before we could get it adopted on most aircraft.

Between the two wars when there was economical technical development going on in connection with civil aeroplanes, many important advances were made, including retractable landing gears, variable pitch propellers, much longer life of the aircraft and much easier maintenance. Undoubtedly war creates a sort of hothouse growth in technical achievement because millions or billions are spent instead of thousands; but it is by no means certain that the resulting gains can be used to the advantage of civil air-craft when the war is over. An exception to this may be in engine design; the last war, for example, having brought about the development of the jet engine.

*

I have already written about the Moth and its variants, but if these were the best known and the most profitable aircraft we produced between the wars, there were of course many others. I think that the main reason why we survived the many fluctuations in trading conditions was to be found in our decision to follow a safe step-by-step policy, taking as few risks as possible. The Dragon was a case in point.

One day Edward Hillman came to discuss the possi-bility of a small airliner. Hillman was a remarkable man. He had been running a bus service of his own, even driving the vehicles himself when he first started. With unbounded energy he built up a sound organization and now had greater ambitions: he wanted to start a London–Paris air service. For this purpose he formed Hillman Airways, which ran successfully until his sudden and premature death. His enthusiasm was contagious, and we at once looked into an eight-seater 'airliner', using two Gipsy Major engines and Tiger Moth extension wings. The fuselage, tail unit, landing gear, controls, etc., were, of course, new. The success of the Dragon design was largely due to Hillman's far-sighted and courageous action in ordering a small fleet of them 'off the drawing board'.

Next, a six-cylinder Gipsy engine was developed from the original four-cylinder, and two of these, still in pursuance of our safe policy in technical advance, were fitted to a more powerful 'plane, which we called the Dragon Rapide. The Rapide was an outstanding case of a design being just right. Arthur Hagg, who was then our chief designer, was largely responsible for it. The 'plane needs no detailed description here because there are today hundreds of Rapides still flying all over the world. It shares with the American D.C.3, or Dakota, the distinction of being the most reliable, useful and easily maintained aeroplane ever made. During its early production before the war the Rapide sold for under four thousand pounds. Now, after nearly thirty years, the same aircraft change hands for about the same amount. But if built today the Rapide would have to have a host of new requirements built into it and would be far heavier, more complex and would cost nearer forty thousand pounds.

There were occasional exceptions to this 'next step' policy. The first of these was the Comet 1 Racer, built in 1934 for the MacRobertson England–Australia Air Race. An all-wood, cantilever monoplane with two of our new Gipsy Six engines, it had the first retractable under-carriage we had made, and also the first variable pitch propellers we had used. Its range was two thousand two hundred miles. We built the Comet Racer because it looked as if American aircraft might be easy winners unless something out of the ordinary were designed. And so, in this case, we were forced to gamble.

We offered the racing Comets at a nominal figure of five thousand pounds each (they naturally cost us far more than this), and we had got orders for three: from Amy and Jim Mollison, Bernard Rubin the millionaire motor racing driver (flown by Jones and Waller), and A. O. Edwards of the Grosvenor House Hotel, whose pilots were Charles Scott and Tom Campbell-Black.

Aeroplanes are seldom ready for delivery on the pro-mised day, but this Comet had to be ready for the day of the race or all the work and time and money we had put into them would be wasted. I don't think any of us would care to live again through the weeks of agony that pre-ceded the start of the race. Economic conditions at the time were unfavourable, the stakes were high, and we were not accustomed to gambling like this. Hubert Broad, our test pilot, was forced to do the work which usually lasted many months in only a few weeks; and instead of prolonged flight tests, he had to limit each to ten or fifteen minutes, landing frequently for a series of minor adjustments. This was the only way to get everything right in the short time available. The effect of this type of testing on many of us, and certainly on me, was to make it difficult to believe that the machine could ever be capable of a really long flight. But this feeling was, of course, purely psychological; the Comets had a thorough if unorthodox testing. By the time we arrived at Mildenhall for the start we were half dead from exhaustion; and yet tremendously excited by the tension that built up during those last days.

There were the usual agonizing last minute adjustments on the eve of the race, and one fairly extensive repair due to a heavy landing which kept tired people working all night. But by dawn of starting day everything was ready, and the three heavily loaded Comets got off all right and disappeared to the south. Many other aircraft were taking part, of course, but we had scarcely had time to glance at them. The one exception was the American Douglas D.C.2 airliner, a very fast and well tried-out machine, and the one real menace to our chances. This was a competitor we could not afford to disregard.

Then came the long and trying wait for news. But what grand news when it arrived! What had seemed impossible had happened, and the months of toil and hope and anxiety were forgotten when we heard that the Comet flown by the Mollisons had reached Baghdad non-stop. But there was plenty of excitement and more anxiety before the end. Scott and Campbell-Black were stuck at Darwin with trouble in one engine. Frank Halford at once showed those wonderful fighting qualities that were evident in all he did. He somehow discovered that a London newspaper had a telephone line 'open' to Australia and got permission to use it. He was soon talking to Scott and heard what the symptoms of the trouble were. It was obviously connected with oil pressure, and Halford realized that it might possibly be only a defective oil pressure gauge that was the cause. He told Scott to go ahead, forget the gauge and give the engine a rather easier time when in the air. Scott and Campbell-Black arrived first at Melbourne and won the ten thousand pounds prize. They had taken seventy hours fifty-nine minutes to cover 11,300 miles—an outstanding feat of skill and endurance.

Our gamble with the Comet Racer, and Halford's own gamble with the oil pressure trouble, had both come off.

*

When we first began manufacturing aircraft at Stag Lane in 1920 there was only one small house near the aerodrome, but as the business expanded houses went up all around us, and ten years later we had to consider seriously a move to a less congested area. For many months we looked for a suitable site, doing a lot of reconnaissance by Moth along most of the main roads leading out of London, the most hopeful being to the north. Eventually we found an area near Hatfield that looked good from the air, a large level area of farmland bordering the main road. The farmer was prepared to sell at a reasonable price. The value of Stag Lane had greatly increased and we were able to sell the aerodrome at a good profit. We retained our works buildings there, and it is still our Engine Company's experimental centre. When Stag Lane aerodrome was sold it was quickly built over and now is part of outer London.

The first to move to Hatfield was the flying side, including the London Aeroplane Club, our own flying section and private owners' lock-ups and aircraft. Suitable buildings for personnel and aircraft were erected, the land was drained, ditches filled in and a good grass aerodrome was soon being used. Although not beautiful, the country around our new aerodrome was very pleasant, and of course it possessed a greater sense of spaciousness than Stag Lane ever had. An architect was needed, for we wanted attractive buildings as well as efficiency. Hearle as Works Manager, in company with several others, motored about the Great West Road district where there was a number of good-looking modern factory buildings. He fixed on one that satisfied all our conditions and found out the name of the architect. We told him our requirements and he produced plans for the various buildings which, even after twenty-five years, are still considered efficient and attractive. At Stag Lane the take-off area had already been reduced to a narrow strip when, with a certain sense of sadness, I made my last take-off in July 1934 and flew the few miles north to Hatfield.

In order to guard against the urban development that had ruined Stag Lane for us, we bought a lot of land adjoining the aerodrome, and much of this was efficiently farmed as a profitable side line. Alan Butler took a great interest in the farm, and with the help of a very able head man he quickly had a grass drying plant in action. A pedigree herd of cattle, pigs and chicken were soon all doing well. There was quite a lot of grass scattered over the farm and week-end shoots have been the rule ever since we settled at Hatfield. The aerodrome itself is usually occupied by rooks, hares, occasionally partridges and pheasants, and more rarely by a flock of golden plovers. Hares have become quite accustomed to the frequent roar of jet aircraft taking off, and merely move aside in a leisurely manner at their approach.

The move to Hatfield was much more than a mere geographical one. By the early 'thirties, the Company was large, well-established and a respected one in the British aircraft industry. After only a decade we could look back on some substantial achievements; and in our new location with new, better-planned buildings, we looked forward with confidence to a great future. Perhaps a more important reason for our optimism was the good team spirit that we had been fortunate enough to possess since the beginning. We all got on well together, and there was a sort of family feeling in all departments which was not only congenial but produced good results. It was quite a family business in the literal meaning of the word, too. At one time I had three sons, a brother, two nephews and a stepson in the firm.

Now this is a situation that is fraught with danger, and one that directors of many firms have to face. In my own case I have made it an invariable rule to show no favours to relatives or friends either in connection with their appointment or their future progress. Once influence or favours are shown trouble starts, and there is no saying where it may end. In the bad old days it was apparently common for the Boss to put his son or other close relative into a soft job and to see that he got advancement whether he was a moron or a genius. All that has changed now, and has probably gone forever. Unless a relative or friend of a director can show real merit and conform strictly to the established rules, it is always best for him to get out as quickly as he can. Also in these days the average shop workers, who are nearly always a good lot, will not stand for this type of favouritism; and they are absolutely right.

None of my relatives or friends who have been or are now with the company has ever suggested I should use any influence on his behalf, and they have retained their jobs on merit alone. Geoffrey and John, for example, were obviously pilots of great skill; and Peter, my surviving son, after doing some years of very useful flying, joined the sales side where his knowledge of French was, and is today, a big asset.

CHAPTER ELEVEN

MOSQUITO

A<small>LL</small> through the 1930s we concentrated on civil air-craft of many types from Moths to airliners, ending with the D.H. Flamingo, the first all-metal airliner we had built. But as the clouds developed over Europe in 1937 and 1938 and conflict with Hitler became almost inevitable, our thoughts turned very reluctantly towards war aircraft.

Our minds naturally went back to the D.H.4 of the 1914 War, the high-speed bomber that could outfly most enemy fighters. We were confident that this formula would be as novel and as vitally needed as it had been before and that, provided we did not permit orthodoxy—especially in the shape of officialdom—to stifle us, we could do better still the second time. Our scheme was to discard every item of equipment that was not essential, design for a two-man crew and *no* rear armament, relying on high speed for defence. We proposed using two Rolls-Royce Merlin engines, the best in the world. A specification and general arrangement drawings were therefore prepared, and we got ready for the next stage. We knew it was not going to be an easy one.

One day in 1937 Walker and I went to the Air Ministry to put forward our project with hope and some pride in our hearts. We outlined our scheme and showed the drawings. They were barely glanced at. Then the bolder of the two officials, addressed us like a schoolmaster and, waving a hand towards our cherished plans, he said:

156

'Forget it. You people haven't produced a war machine for years, and if you want to do so now you must start on something quite simple—perhaps design a wing for an experimental plane.'

He paused for a moment and then suddenly came out with an idea which he obviously thought was a winner.

'As a matter of fact that's not a bad idea. We've got one coming along, and you may be able to help us on this little job. It's called "The Ape".'

I looked at him half in anger and half in resigned despair, and nearly said, 'Why produce another?'

In spite of this, we continued work on the design, being confident of the final decision. All members of our technical staff were enthusiastic about the project. Ronald E. Bishop had been our chief designer for some years and was in charge of the team ably assisted by C. T. Wilkins, now a director and Chief Designer of our Aircraft Company, Richard M. Clarkson, head of the aerodynamics section and Robert Harper head of the stress section. Bishop and many others in the technical branch had come to us as students in our Technical School, and now held important positions in various departments. Eventually something happened that was to have far-reaching and beneficial results on the conduct of the future war in the air. Air Marshal Sir Wilfrid Freeman was appointed Chief Executive at the Air Ministry. I had known Freeman since the early days of the 1914 War and had always liked him. He was far more than a very successful Air Force officer, he had technical knowledge much above the average, and in discussion was helpful and without bias. I had stayed a short time at his headquarters in France in 1916 when he was in charge of a squadron of D.H.4s and I felt he would appreciate our wish to build a modern version of that successful machine. It needed only one meeting with this wise and far-sighted man to discuss our plans and to get his full approval and blessing for the Mosquito.

But if it had been accepted when we first approached the Air Ministry, six months of precious time could have been saved.

The most significant feature of the Mosquito, of course, was its all-wood construction. The last 'all wood' airliner we had built was the Albatross, probably the largest airliner of high performance to be made of this material. The type of construction was similar to the successful racing Comet and its lines were extremely clean and attractive, everything possible being done to reduce 'drag'. It was powered by four of our newly designed Gipsy Twelve engines with a new scheme of ducted air cooling. The Albatross was on the London–Paris service for a short time, but production and development of this airliner, and also of the Flamingo and Moth Minor, were ended by the war. There were very good reasons why we should use wood for the Mosquito, too. Our experience had been chiefly with advanced wood structure, there were thousands of skilled woodworkers readily available, the stocks of aluminium alloy sheet metal were already allotted. Finally, and most important, we estimated that a year could be saved in production due to the simplicity of wood construction as compared with metal. There is little difference in the weight of wood or metal aircraft when dealing with structures of the size of the Mosquito. All this gave us a wonderful opportunity to make an outstanding war aeroplane in almost record time.

The final design and building of the prototype was moved from Hatfield to Salisbury Hall, about five miles away, for safety during air raids. Salisbury Hall is an old country mansion surrounded by a moat, and is of historical and romantic interest.

Amongst many Salisbury Hall traditions was one that claimed that a smaller building on the side of the moat had been the temporary home of Nell Gwynne. The carving on the staircase posts was carefully boxed in by us because it was said to be of great age and value. The same applied to some very old wallpaper in certain rooms. Altogether it was a house of romantic charm and seemingly far removed from the design and building of a modern war aircraft. We left Salisbury Hall after the war and it started to fall into decay, but fortunately a Mrs. Goldsmith came upon the house one day and told her husband of its charm. Mr. Goldsmith, an artist, and his wife and young family now occupy the house, and to them it has been a labour of love to repair the ravages of time and weather in house and garden and restore its dignity and charm. It is now listed as an 'Ancient Monument' and has also provided a happy ending to the Mosquito story. The prototype Mosquito, born there in 1940, has gone back to its original home and can be seen there today.

The design staff worked in the house, and sheds were erected in the grounds for assembling the prototype. These were ideal conditions, and we felt we were working in a small world of our own with the minimum of interference. To watch a new design take shape day by day is always absorbing and exciting. Only those with special permits were allowed to see the work in progress, and we were worried by fewer official visits than usual, although there was one unofficial one. Whether by accident or design we never knew, but a German spy was parachuted one night and landed quite near by. He must have been inefficient at his job because he was captured within a few hours and before he had even been able to collect useful information. He was quickly disposed of in the usual way.

The first order for Mosquitoes was received on March 1, 1940. It was for fifty bombers to be built 'off the drawing board'. But in May we were instructed to stop work on the order and concentrate all our resources on repairing Hurricanes and Merlin engines. This followed on Dunkirk and it was thought that attempted invasion of England was imminent. We therefore suggested that the hundreds of

Tiger Moth trainers might play a part if an enemy landing was attempted, and we designed special bomb racks to carry eight 20-lb. bombs per aircraft. One thousand five hundred sets were made ready, but were never needed.

By persistently worrying the officials who stopped Mosquito work we eventually got it reinstated in July. We had never stopped work entirely, and not much time was lost.

When the first Mosquito was nearly finished, a high ranking officer of the Royal Air Force came to see it, and in the course of conversation told me of the newly developed marvels of Radar, explaining that, if fitted to the Mosquito, it would enable the pilot to find another aircraft even at night or in fog. I admit that I thought this was exaggeration, but didn't say so. How wrong I had been was soon to be demonstrated when night fighter Mosquitoes were fitted with Radar.

The Mosquito embodied several new design features. The radiators for the Merlin engines were placed in the wings on both sides between the engine and fuselage. The exit of the air was under the wing. This considerably reduced resistance as compared with an external radiator. Experiments were made with the exit shape of the engine exhausts and led to appreciable forward thrust being obtained. The fuselage was formed by a balsa wood filling between an inner and outer skin of plywood. This made a light, stiff and stable structure with no need for further stiffening. A feature that helped greatly in construction was the division of the fuselage into two half sections down the top and bottom lines of the whole length. This allowed nearly all the equipment, controls, wiring, instruments, etc., to be installed with much greater ease. The usual sight of men groping about to do this work with only legs and part of a bottom sticking out of the normal one-piece fuselage gave way to far greater ease of work and much reduction in time taken. The wing structure had to be designed so that 500-odd gallons of fuel could be carried in tanks in the space between structure members. The top and bottom wing skins were each formed by two layers of three-ply separated by long stiffening 'stringers' running the whole span of the wings. We had for some years used rubber blocks in compression for landing gear shock absorbers because they enabled a simpler, less expensive gear to be used free of costly machining and complex oil damping. This same method was applied to the Mosquito landing gear with complete success.

When the main work on the plane was finished it was disassembled and taken to a small and inconspicuous shed on Hatfield Aerodrome where the finishing touches were carried out. The shed was only large enough to take one Mosquito, and this tended to make the plane look far bigger than it was. But, as always happens, when hauled out on to the aerodrome it looked absurdly small, and seemed to be largely made up of engines and propellers.

Because the Mosquito was a very new type, and also because we had fought hard for the form it was to take, everyone's feelings before the first trial flight were tense. I suppose that, subconsciously at least, I was certain that we had in the Mosquito a real war-winning 'plane, but this did not prevent me from fretting about the multitude of things that could go wrong. I was, after all, about to be the spectator of what I suspected was to be the most momentous take-off of any of our 'planes.

My son Geoffrey, who had flown as a baby in his mother's arms in my first aircraft, was to be the pilot. He had followed the construction of the 'plane right from the beginning and was to be responsible for all the subsequent testing.

The Aerodynamics Department had worked out the performance of take-off run, rate of climb, high speed and stall speed, as had been done on all previous 'planes in the past years. This data of performance was seldom more than

2 per cent or 3 per cent at variance from the measured figures during actual test flying. Geoffrey therefore knew what to expect even on the first flight. The Rolls-Royce Merlin engines were given the usual thorough test run, and Geoffrey climbed into the pilot's seat; John Walker, the chief of the Engine Installation Department, took the seat at his side and slightly to the rear.

Many taxiing runs were made to test ground control, landing gear and tail skid, the length and speed of each run being increased until take-off seemed very near. Then Geoffrey taxied back to the main group who were eagerly waiting for news. He said all was well and that he would take her into the air.

The great moment had come after only eleven months from the start of the design of the fastest aeroplane we had ever built—a speed record in itself. The tense excitement of the many watchers showed itself in various ways. We all tried to look and act normally, but I kept walking back to my car to open and shut the door quite without reason, while others walked off a short way and returned more quickly. It was a great relief when I heard the engines opened up fully with the 'plane held back by the wheel brakes. The engine roar continued as the brakes were suddenly released. The Mosquito gathered speed rapidly, the power to weight ratio being very high, and it lifted easily and was truly air-borne on its first flight. As it continued its steady course, the pent-up feelings of awful anxiety gave way to relief and great hopes for the future.

If a new 'plane is up for about fifteen minutes on a first flight, the watchers can feel fairly certain that nothing much is wrong with the controls or trim. Geoffrey was up for nearly thirty minutes and then reappeared, circled and came in to make a perfect landing. When he climbed out we all surrounded him to ask 'how it went'. His brief verbal report was that only minor work and adjustments were required.

The serious test flying, which includes careful measurements of performance, control, stability, functioning of the constant speed propellers, engine cooling, oil cooling, pilot's comfort, especially at altitude, cockpit heating and pressure, effect of 'cannon' firing, petrol consumption, and so on were all dealt with at maximum speed.

The Mosquito, being the most versatile warplane ever made, soon took on the different roles of bomber, photo reconnaissance 'plane, fighter (both night and day), high altitude fighter, a carrier for a six-pounder gun. The fighter carried four 20-mm. cannon in the nose under the cockpit and four machine-guns. The bomber version, designed for four 250-lb. bombs, was soon carrying twice that load, and in 1944 carried the 4,000-lb. bomb. 'Drop' tanks under the wings increased the range steadily and Rolls-Royce never failed to get more power out of the wonderful Merlin engines when this was needed.

Speed is always difficult to measure accurately, due to possible instrument error or position of the pitot head which conveys the pressure of air through long pipe lines to the instrument in the cockpit, so we 'borrowed' a Spitfire and pilot to fly alongside the Mosquito and note the difference in speed. It was fairly easy for both pilots to agree on the difference, which could not be great. After several tests it was agreed tnat the Mosquito was about twenty miles per hour faster than the Spitfire. This was better than estimate, and better than anyone had anticipated.

The second Mosquito, also built at Salisbury Hall, was the first fighter-bomber version. In order to save the month required for taking it to pieces, transporting to Hatfield and re-assembling, it was wheeled to a field at the back of Salisbury Hall which Geoffrey had inspected and passed as a just possible take-off ground. The operation was successful and the 'plane landed safely at Hatfield with Fred Plumb, who was in charge of construction, in the second seat.

The main testing had been completed with very few snags, and Geoffrey had got thoroughly familiar with the 'plane. The time had come for an official demonstration, and in May 1941 invitations were sent to many top ranking members of the Ministry, including, of course, Lord Beaverbrook, who was then in charge of aircraft production. Officers of the Royal Air Force were also invited, and I was glad to welcome Sir Wilfrid Freeman, who had made the Mosquito possible in spite of strong opposition from many members of the Air Ministry and also the Air Force, including Bomber Command. The Mosquito had, for some time, been known at the Air Ministry as 'Freeman's Folly', and it was good to know that he was to see his foresight and unshaken belief in the Mosquito justified in a very practical, even sensational, demonstration.

Geoffrey's demonstration was spectacular. It included all known—and a few unknown—evolutions. Slow and full speed runs were made over the aerodrome only a few feet above the ground. From a full speed run a vertical climb took the Mosquito up to three thousand feet or more. Loops, rolls, dives, showed convincingly the easy and safe handling qualities. He then did this demonstration over again but with one propeller feathered and stationary, ending with a soft landing in a relatively short distance. Even the least demonstrative of the visitors, as well as those who had previously been 'anti' Mosquito, were enthusiastic about this practical demonstration. We pointed out the main features: Span 54 feet, length 44.5 feet, total weight 22,587 lb., speed 425 miles per hour at 30,000 feet. And there were other vital features quite as important as the performance but far less obvious. Four to five Mosquitoes could be built for one of the heavy bombers, thus saving enormous effort, expense and man-hours. It carried a crew of only two, thus saving greater sums in training, and also saving lives. It was faster than any fighter, in fact it was the fastest warplane in the world for two and a half years. It could fill the role of any of the many military 'planes then existing. All these claims were fully borne out when the Mosquito went into actual Royal Air Force service in September 1941.

A vast production of Mosquitoes was now started and we were asked to arrange for 'dispersal' as far as possible. Soon there were four hundred sub-contractors working on the various units, chiefly cabinet makers, furniture factories, our own factories at Hatfield and Leavesden, and all conceivable concerns, large and small. Drawings and schedules—there were ten thousand to make a complete set—were sent to our Canadian and Australian factories, and they also started on production.

The adaptability of the Mosquito was a blessing and a curse, because it led to the total number of forty-three types or 'Marks' of the 'plane. The differences were, in some cases, small, but even so, meant far greater problems in production and also in spares. Precise performances of a warplane can never be finalized. Speed is constantly being increased and so is rate of climb, maximum height, load, range, petrol and ammunition capacity, and a host of minor improvements, all in order to outclass the enemy. The basic design of the 'plane remained more or less constant, as did the basic design of the Rolls-Royce Merlin engine, but the engine was called upon to give more and more power until by the end of the war it was developing more than twice the power of the original engine.

It would be impossible to tell of all the successes (and the failures) of the Mosquito during its Service life in the Royal Air Force. A lot has been brilliantly told in the book by Edward Bishop entitled *The Wooden Wonder*, but I have added at the end of this book[1] some typical cases from my brother, Hereward's, reports, made while he was acting as liaison man between Hatfield and the various Royal Air Force squadrons using Mosquitoes. Hereward's

[1] See Appendix I.

background and experience made him particularly suitable for this job. He had taken an engineering degree before the first war, had flown with the R.F.C. in it—incidentally earning a D.S.O.—and after a period in Spain as the company's representative had joined us in 1927, later managing our Australian branch. A first-class engineer, he has never shown any desire to become a designer, except in connection with one of his main hobbies, which is designing, and making, particularly fine furniture.

Hereward travelled to every country where Mosquito squadrons were operating, and his reports cover some two hundred foolscap pages. If these were read by the uninitiated they could be excused for saying 'This sounds like a damned awful aeroplane'. But the same would be said of similar reports on *any* war aeroplane. It is simply that the many different hazards that any warplane is subjected to make it look hopelessly bad.

The builders of any warplane, or, in fact of any war equipment, would like to have much more time for design and also for testing, but time is a vital factor in war. When the first few Mosquitoes had been given the normal tests it was urgently wanted for operation by the Royal Air Force. This same urgency applies to all warplanes and many defects show up due to the necessity of sending machines out before they can be really ready. If delayed until they were nearly perfect they would never be sent at all. And obviously, this also applies to aero engines.

The production of all war equipment eventually depends on the man-hours available and therefore if any article of equipment can be simplified or made smaller, or of easily worked materials, more of it can be made for a given number of man-hours. This is where the Mosquito scored heavily. It could carry a greater load of bombs per man-hour of work than the big bombers, and, of course, at a much higher speed, and only needed a crew of two instead of from five to eight. To attain this result we had had to fight hard, we were constantly urged during design, for example, to equip it with rear defence, but we consistently refused because it would have led to a heavier and slower aircraft. For rear defence we had relied entirely on high speed as in the case of the D.H.4. The proof that we were justified was demonstrated by the performance of the Mosquito in actual war operations.

During the war we had expanded at Hatfield as little as possible, largely making use of sub-contractors for producing the various units for Mosquitoes. At peak production, and including sub-contractors, there was a total of seventy-five thousand people working on our wartime products. Of the seven thousand seven hundred and eighty-one Mosquitoes produced, the majority were made in Britain and the rest in Canada and Australia.

CHAPTER TWELVE

THE COMET AND AFTER

THE principle of jet propulsion has been known for a great number of years, but it was not until just before the war that vague rumours were heard about practical jet engines. The Germans were the first to put into production a jet engine in an aeroplane, the Messerschmitt 262. It was a desperate effort to counter our devastating bombing raids, but their engine was only in the experimental stage and hopelessly unreliable. After the war a German fighter pilot admitted that when the ME.262 went into service in 1944 it killed more Germans than the enemy.

We heard that Whittle had a jet engine working and that it would soon be fitted into an aeroplane. Later, some of us, including Frank Halford, our engine designer, flew up to Cranwell where the Whittle engine was being flown in a specially built Gloster monoplane, and we witnessed one of the earliest flights using jet propulsion. The take-off run was very long and the flight was short, but it clearly demonstrated the possibility of a completely new era in flying. Here was an impressive new development and we were far from being indifferent to it but we all knew that much development work would be necessary in order to build a reliable engine suitable for a fighter aeroplane.

Halford was enthusiastic about the engine, and in 1940 was invited to design a production jet engine of greater thrust, suitable for a jet fighter, and it was decided that Bishop, our chief designer, should at the same time get out plans for a single-seater fighter 'plane. The result of the combined effort was the Vampire, powered by the Goblin jet engine. It was a highly successful aeroplane that went into large scale production, and was supplied to various countries overseas in big numbers. In 1947 John Cunningham gained the 100-km. closed circuit record on a Vampire at a speed of 496.88 m.p.h. In 1948 he flew a Ghost-engined Vampire to a (then) record height of 59,446 feet. The Vampire was followed by the Venom, similar in design, but powered by the larger Ghost jet engine developed from the Goblin. There were several versions, one being the Sea Venom, used on aircraft carriers by the Royal Navy.

It was clear that jet propulsion had opened a new era in flying, and when, towards the end of the war, our thoughts naturally turned to consider the form that civil aircraft were likely to take, jet propulsion had to be seriously considered. The Americans had got a long way ahead with piston-engined aircraft because they had concentrated largely on military transports while Britain had been concerned more with fighters and light bombers. Pilots of jet fighters commented not only on their higher performance in speed and climb, but also on the notable lack of vibration and relative lack of noise.

In order to reduce air resistance still further, designers were looking into the possibility of doing away with the tail unit and obtaining control and stability from sweptback wings with 'elevons', swept wings being necessary in any case for higher speeds. We thought this might also have a bearing on the design of a jet airliner.

To test the idea in the most practical way we decided to make a small experimental, single-seat, tailless monoplane with a Goblin jet engine. This was the D.H.108. Geoffrey made the first flight, and after the usual adjustments and minor modifications he continued the testing, and while not being entirely satisfied with the stability, he thought it was capable of very high speeds. Week after

169

week he cautiously increased speed as he gained more experience with each flight. But the scheme of swept-back wings and elevons had at least one disadvantage. When landing the elevons were 'up' in order to depress the wing tips and increase the angle of incidence, but this also had the effect of reducing the effective span of the wings due to the loss of lift of the outboard sections, thus increasing the landing speed.

Eventually Geoffrey felt pretty certain that the machine had a chance of breaking the world speed record, which then stood at 616 miles per hour. It was arranged that he should try for the record in a few days' time, and I saw him off on a final test flight from Hatfield on the evening of September 27, 1946. I was rung up at home later in the evening with the news that he was long overdue, and that an aeroplane was reported to have 'exploded' over the Thames Estuary. I dreaded the worst. At low tide next day wreckage was reported on the mud flats near Egypt Bay, just north of the village of Cliffe and north-east of Gravesend. Geoffrey's body was not found for several days, and then much further down the river.

Apart from the numbing shock of the tragedy to Louie and me and close relatives, a deep gloom was cast over all at Hatfield and our other factories, and his many friends in the industry. Geoffrey had always been loved because of his natural, intimate, almost casual manner, his great sense of humour and his outstanding skill in flying.

Three years earlier John had been piloting a Mosquito among scattered clouds when there was a collision from which there had been no survivors. Words are utterly inadequate to describe the sense of loss and shock from such tragedies, and poor Louie never really got over them. After John's death she had convinced herself that no harm could come to Geoffrey, whatever he did, which made this second disaster all the more terrible for her.

We were thankful for two thoughts that to some extent

helped to soften our anguish. Geoffrey and John had died instantaneously, and both had died doing the work they loved above all else. They were both dedicated to flying, and Geoffrey used to worry because, although quite young, he felt that a day would come when he would be too old for test flying and he could think of nothing else he wanted to do. Even his holidays were taken rather reluctantly—it meant being away from flying—but he loved the sea and surfing and swimming. At home at week-ends he stoked up his scale model steam engines, some of which he had had at school, and I am sure he was happier when his face and hands were blackened by coal dust and smoke and oil. He kept fit by playing squash at Hatfield, and he liked a party with congenial friends, but was like me in hating any sort of formal or social function, and was shy with strangers. He could lose himself at an occasional wild party, and a small amount of alcohol would sometimes lay him out, but next morning he would be eager for work with no trace of 'hangover'.

Geoffrey and John had spent many happy days at Tewin, a little village, not far from Hatfield, where they lived during some of the war years, and it is in Tewin Church-yard that they are buried.

In the main entrance hall at Hatfield is a plaque of Geoffrey and the wording reads:

'He lost his life while flying at a speed greater than had previously been attained by man.'

In spite of many months of concentrated examination of wreckage by the best brains, the cause of the break-up of the 108 was never established. Every increase of speed leads inevitably to new problems of stability and control, and during the 108 tests Geoffrey had formed the definite opinion that it was not advisable to do away with the tail unit for more normal types of aircraft until far more data was available.

171

We were living at Harpenden at the time of Geoffrey's death. Louie was far from well and was anxious to get back amongst her old friends at Stanmore where we had lived for many years. At last we heard of a house for sale, it was suitable and we bought it in 1946. Here Louie was happier, but did not really improve. The doctors said it was a nervous breakdown, but as she became steadily worse I got a noted physician to see her. After many and various treatments he told me that she had cancer and that nothing could be done. Louie died at home a few weeks later, due, I believe, to the tragic losses of John and Geoffrey as much as to physical causes. She too, is buried in Tewin Churchyard.

*

While in Canada and America testing Mosquitoes during the war Geoffrey had seen my cousins Olivia de Havilland and Joan Fontaine, and I was naturally anxious to meet them for the first time when they came to this country soon after the war was over. I had seen them on the screen in the films made early in their careers, and was impressed by their talent for acting and their strikingly good looks. They must have inherited their ability for good acting from their mother, who had been successful on the stage in Shakespearian plays, for I have never heard of an actress or actor, good or bad, in the de Havilland family. Olivia and Joan showed real kindness in sending us regularly every month luxuries which we could not get here during the war.

In the 1950s Joan came to England to take part in the film *Ivanhoe* and invited my wife and me and Peter's wife to Elstree to see some of the 'shooting' of the picture. A lot of the 'outside' scenes were 'shot' in a well-roofed studio. The extensive background was canvas painted blue to represent sky (they said as it rained nearly every day in England they had to work inside). Joan took us to lunch in the studio restaurant and we returned to see more filming. After being introduced to a few famous stars we left. It had been a new and interesting experience.

Olivia's first part in a big film was as Melanie in *Gone With the Wind* in which she was brilliant and which launched her on a successful film career. She had previously been directed by Max Reinhardt in the Shakespearian play, *Midsummer Night's Dream,* taking the part of Hermia. Her favourite parts in her various films were Melanie, Virginia in *The Snake Pit* and Catherine in *The Heiress.* Olivia now lives in France and we see her on some of her visits to England. She is married to M. Pierre Galante.

Joan's first big film was *Rebecca.* She told me her favourite parts were in *Letter from an Unknown Woman, The Constant Nymph* and *Rebecca.* She is now on the stage and says she would like to be known one day as a stage actress rather than as a 'cinema queen'. Olivia and Joan both learnt to fly on light 'planes in America and were impressed when they visited Hatfield and were taken for jet fighter flights.

*

A few years before the war a student named John Cunningham had entered our Technical School and, later, having learnt to fly, he joined No. 604 Squadron of the Auxiliary Air Force, and also became one of our test pilots. Just before the war we had made a light two-seater monoplane, known as the Moth Minor, fitted with a new Gipsy Minor engine, and it was hoped to develop this Moth Minor into a really low priced private owners' 'plane. I had made the first test flights—incidentally the last 'first' test flights I was to make—and Geoffrey and John Cunningham were completing the tests, including spinning trials. There was something rather unusual about these spins. One day they started a spin, wisely from a good

173

height, and after several turns of the spin they were somewhat concerned to find they could not stop it. This test was to find out the extreme aft limit of the c.g. (centre of gravity), and this position had been rather overdone intentionally. After losing a few thousand feet Geoffrey told John to bale out, and then left the aircraft himself. It was their first parachute jump. They both landed safely, having watched the Moth Minor crash in open country not far away. Later a fairly simple modification rectified the fault so that recovery was certain and easy. The war put an end to further development of the Moth Minor. Then John Cunningham was called up for service with the Royal Air Force, and before very long was flying Beaufighters against enemy night bombers with great success. When the night fighter Mosquito was available he became an outstanding night fighter pilot, destroying a great many enemy aircraft. He maintained that his night sight was average and had little bearing on his successes, which were due to the efficient use of radar and other technical aids and a relatively long experience of night flying. The story of his brilliantly successful service as a night fighter pilot has been told in the book *Night Fighter*[1] by two of the principal members of his crew. Our thoughts naturally turned to John Cunningham as a successor to Geoffrey as chief test pilot, and he was ready to accept if we could get his release from the Royal Air Force. We were able to arrange this, and he rejoined us in 1946 as chief pilot and controller of flying at Hatfield and our associated companies.

John Derry had been a good demonstration pilot before Geoffrey was killed, and became a brilliant pilot of jet fighters. He was one of the first of our pilots to do 'sonic bangs' on the fighter which later became the Sea Vixen and which is now a standard Naval fighter of high performance. But Derry's first brilliant achievement was to

[1] *Night Fighter* by Rawnsley and Wright, published by Collins.

fly a re-built D.H.108 (similar to the one on which Geoffrey made his last flight), and to show its capabilities of high speed. This was done on a 100-km. closed circuit and Derry averaged 605·23 miles per hour, setting up an international record which stood for some years.

John Derry's end was a terrible tragedy. He had been demonstrating the D.H.110 at the Farnborough Display in 1952 and every day had made several 'sonic bangs'. He came down quite low in a steep dive and when doing a turn a wing failed. It had presumably been overstrained previously. A complete break-up followed and the two jet engines were hurled into the crowded spectators, killing twenty-eight people. Derry and his observer, Tony Richards, were killed in a few seconds.

Every increase in speed—in this case a big increase—creates more problems. Why try and go faster? people ask. The answer is that in aviation, if you don't you are soon left far behind. Speed is the main advantage flying has to offer, and as long as people want to travel from place to place, they will continue to want to do so as quickly as possible.

This is one of the few invariable rules of human behaviour.

John Cunningham's work has carried him to most countries in the world, and he is well known not only as a test pilot of outstanding ability, but as a person of great natural charm. All this has inevitably led to publicity which he considers somewhat unbalanced. No pilot of an airliner can perform without a co-pilot and crew in whom he has absolute confidence, but who seldom share the publicity. John has his chosen co-pilots, and at least one of these, Peter Bugge, was a very successful night fighter pilot in the war at the same time as John. Peter Wilson is another test pilot who has done a great amount of Comet and other flying. Pilot, co-pilot, engineer and navigator have for years worked together as a team as near perfect as it is possible to make it. John Cunningham is certainly not the type who would ever seek publicity, but no man or woman can govern the publicity they receive, for that is in the hands of the Press reporters who are always looking for the unusual and sensational, and above all the colourful personality. John is test pilot, demonstration pilot, salesman and ambassador, all in one, and has made some sensational flights. He can do thousands of miles for many days, and at the end of the flight can be charming, unruffled and apparently as fresh as ever when discussing points raised by a host of officials, Pressmen and others. He became a director of our Aircraft Company, together with C. T. Wilkins, our Chief Designer, in 1958.

It was John, of course, who was mainly responsible for the difficult and highly specialized testing of the Comet airliner. We first gave consideration to the Comet project in the closing stages of the war. It was clear that, by reason of her concentration on transport and bombing aircraft during the war, America would have a big lead when the inevitable competition for long-distance airliners began in peacetime. It was no use following what they were doing and making something *slightly* better; our only chance, in contradiction to our old step-by-step policy was to make one great leap and thus gain a lead which would take years to whittle down. The answer seemed to lie in the jet engine, in which we had a big lead over America. We knew that jet fighters were vibrationless and far less noisy for passengers and crew, and therefore the solution of the airliner problem seemed obvious—an aircraft fitted with four jet engines. Our Engine Company had developed the Ghost jet engine for the Venom, and we decided to design the aeroplane round four of these engines, each giving 5,000 lb. thrust. We knew the project would be more difficult than normal designs as several entirely new problems would have to be worked out. Bishop, who had been largely responsible for our jet fighters, started making

176

layouts of a jet airliner. These layouts of a new type usually take about six months before even the general arrangement is more or less complete. One of the early schemes had tail booms similar to the Vampire, with three engines in the tail, but eventually it came back to a fairly orthodox design with the four jet engines partially buried in the wings.

Towards the end of the war I had been a member of the Second Brabazon Committee. These Committees had been formed under Lord Brabazon to discuss and advise on the types of civil aircraft likely to be required after the war. I have never had much faith in committees, but I think these were better than some, in spite of my being a member. One of the types recommended was a jet mail carrier capable of crossing the Atlantic. In our Comet layouts we tended to consider it primarily as a passenger airliner with mail taking second place. British Overseas Airways were very much in favour of the proposed jet airliner, and after discussion with them and with the Air Ministry they placed an order for twenty-four Comets. We were now in constant touch with B.O.A.C. regarding special requirements, equipment and performance generally.

The Mosquito had been built 'off the drawing board', and we proposed to do the same with the Comet. The chief and very important advantage of this is the great saving in time as against the older method of first building a prototype which is thoroughly tested and 'got right' before production starts. This latter method may sound more rational but, in practice, the testing may go on for years for it is always possible to find something that requires modification. Another point which is sometimes forgotten is that if it is known that a prototype is to be made, the design office people are very much inclined to risk trying something new and too experimental in the knowledge that if it fails it can easily be changed or modified before production starts. They are far less inclined to take these risks if production on a number of aircraft is to start right away. In this case we had quite enough new problems to tackle without adding unnecessary ones.

We have found the 'off the drawing board' aircraft have fewer 'teething' troubles and snags due to too clever ideas, and there is obviously the great saving in time which in itself is of untold value. As aircraft increase in size and cost the time and money involved in first building and testing a prototype is prohibitive and runs into millions of money and years of time. But this applies only to fairly orthodox planes that follow reasonably closely a tried-out type. In the case of something very new, like a supersonic airliner, it would be prudent to build and thoroughly test a prototype before going into production.

The general layout of the Comet airliner was finished in 1947. I had spent many hours poring over Bishop's drawing board, sometimes making suggestions and discussing the design generally. From the early days at Stag Lane and at Airco we never had formal meetings on design matters but only informal talks, often at lunch or at tea-time, and seldom with more than three or four present. This worked well until aircraft became bigger and more complex, when, rather reluctantly, we had to hold larger meetings owing to the number of departments and people involved. The trouble with a big meeting is that some people talk too much because they like talking, and others talk too little because they are shy in a crowd.

One of the big differences in designing a military aircraft compared with a civil type is the question of the length of life required from each. In the hazards of war the life of a military aircraft may be only a few hours and seldom reaches the hundreds, but a modern airliner must have a safe life of 30,000 hours. Easy maintenance is desirable in a military type, but it is essential in an airliner. For these and many other reasons the problems of design of the two types are very different.

178

While production of twenty Comets was being planned, the first of these was speeded up by a lot of work being done in the experimental department, so that the first Comet was ready for test flight in July 1949. The first trial flight was made on July 27, and that happens to be the date of John Cunningham's birthday, and also of mine. Some people have asked how it came about that the first flight was made on this day, and I have always had to say I do not know. Recently I asked John whether it was 'fixed' that way or was mere coincidence. John said that, strange as it may seem, it *was* pure coincidence. The second Comet almost made its initial flight on July 27 of the following year, and although this was also called coincidence, I think it very probable that a few final 'adjustments' were found to be desirable!

The first flight of a new design is, for the spectators as well as for the crew, a mixture of great interest, some anxiety and some excitement, but as no one wishes to show any feelings at all, they always look like a group of bored lookers-on, while probably seething inside with excitement. With the minimum load and with only a small amount of fuel, two or three taxiing runs were made to test ground steering and braking. John Cunningham then did a short hop to get an idea of trim and control, and finding all was well, took the Comet into the air on its maiden flight. The eventful career of the first of all jet airliners had commenced.

Testing a modern aircraft is an arduous and exacting job. Hundreds of flights are made, each flight being carefully planned to give specific information. In between flights, adjustments and small modifications are made. The cabin has only a few seats and is unfurnished, but is full of all kinds of instruments for measuring every aspect of performance. Testing a new type like the Comet usually takes about a year, and when the makers are as satisfied as they are ever likely to be—the technical staff would probably like another year or two—the aircraft is handed over to the airline operator who does a long series of route testing and pilot training flights before it goes into service. It has, of course, been designed to comply with the conditions laid down internationally dealing with strength, control, stability, fire risk and performance, and it must obtain a Certificate of Airworthiness before being handed over.

The Comet started airline service in May 1952 and was at once acclaimed as the creator of an entirely new form of travel. The main reasons why the jet airliner is so much in advance of the piston-engined aeroplane in its appeal to passengers and crew are: (1) It is nearly twice as fast; (2) It has negligible vibration, and far less noise; (3) It flies high enough to be above most cloud and air disturbance. All this adds up to far greater comfort in travel.

The initial success of the Comet carried on for nearly two years, with regular services to South Africa, India, and the Far East, and a great future seemed assured. And then a Comet took off from Rome Airport in January 1954 and disappeared shortly afterwards, near Elba, obviously into the sea. All remaining Comets were minutely inspected before flying was resumed on March 23, 1954. Various theories had been suggested as the cause of the disaster—collision with another aircraft, sabotage, pilot's black-out, engine failure, but nothing that could be substantiated. Another Comet took off from Rome in April, and this one also disappeared, near Naples, not far from the site of the first. Comets were again withdrawn from service.

Here was an almost unbelievable coincidence. Comets were flying to almost all parts of the world and yet the two failures occurred within a relatively few miles of each other. In all, fifty-six passengers and crew were killed, fortunately suddenly. There were no survivors and no reliable witnesses. The material loss to B.O.A.C. and ourselves amounted to many millions. But to many of us it was the shattering blow of sudden and complete failure following on notable achievement that was the hardest to bear. The whole nation had formed an affectionate regard for the Comet, and we had failed.

Looking back, I think most of us at Hatfield were— perhaps fortunately—too numbed to realize fully the vast difficulties that lay ahead. On the technical side we felt that it must be possible to seek out and remedy the unknown fault in a short time. The idea of giving up the Comet was never seriously contemplated. It had just got to be made right. On the personal side my second wife, Joan, felt the shock as much as I did, but was consistently encouraging and I was thankful to have her companionship during the devastating time ahead.

The Air Ministry were most helpful in making available research and test facilities at Farnborough. Sir Miles Thomas, always a good friend, and all members of the B.O.A.C. gave us their full co-operation in spite of their tragic disappointment and great material loss. The Royal Navy started the immensely difficult task of salving the wreckage of the first Comet, a task that was to be the first practical step in solving the mystery. It is impossible to over-emphasize the achievement of the Royal Navy in overcoming the vast difficulties involved, devising new and largely untried equipment, contending with all types of weather conditions and carrying on month after month until complete success was assured. Hard work and great patience resulted in the essential parts of the aircraft being recovered. These were sent to the Royal Aircraft Establishment at Farnborough where the almost impossible task of identifying hundreds of pieces of battered metal and placing them in their correct relative positions progressed for many months. Many other tests were carried out at Farnborough, including the building in record time of a water tank to take a complete Comet fuselage for pressure testing. At Hatfield we had previously tested a section of fuselage in a pressure chamber using air in order to establish the ultimate strength, and had the expected failure of the fuselage. But the damage done to the rest of the structure and to the testing equipment was considerable. This was, of course, due to the fact that air, being compressible, gives the effect of an exploding bomb when suddenly released. Water, being incompressible, cannot cause an explosion but makes only a small rent in the structure, and therefore we built a concrete water tank and continued the tests in this. At Farnborough they had built a much larger tank so that the whole fuselage (instead of a section) could be tested. At this time the fuselage was certainly no more suspect than any other part. Wings, tailplane, rudder and elevators from a Comet that had done about the same number of flying hours had been tested, had passed the test and been found to be up to strength. In normal flying, air is *gradually* pumped into the pressure cabin section of the Comet fuselage until it reaches a maximum of $8\frac{1}{4}$ lb. per square inch as the aircraft climbs to cruising altitude— about 40,000 feet—but equivalent to only 8,000 feet in the cabin. On descending at the end of the flight the pressure is *gradually* reduced to zero. These conditions were represented in the tank test except that the duration of the flight, not being an important factor, was neglected so that the effect of many hours of flying could be reduced to minutes.

One day Bishop and I flew over to Farnborough to see how the tests were progressing. Sir Arnold Hall was then Superintendent of the Royal Aircraft Establishment and had organized with his staff the vast job of testing out the wreckage, building the tank and doing much other work in a miraculously short time. We were talking in his office when he was rung up and told that the pressure cabin in the tank had failed after a period representing nine thousand hours' normal flying. We went at once to examine the failure, and found a rent in the side of the cabin which appeared to start from a rivet at the corner of a window-frame. The rent was repaired and the test resumed, and a similar failure occurred, again starting at the corner of a window-frame. At last, after the expenditure of an enormous amount of time and money, we had reached the end of the trail. There was definite evidence of weakness in the cabin structure.

It was obviously an enormous relief to know the cause of the previous disasters, but it also seemed to challenge our technical design ability. Why had we not found this weakness during our own extensive tests? I believe the brief answer to this complex question is that, although much was known about metal fatigue, not *enough* was known by anyone anywhere. Fatigue had been usually associated with high periods of vibration as in the moving parts of a piston engine, or the reversal loads in a wing in turbulent air, but not, or only very vaguely, in a case like the slow rise and fall of pressure in a cabin. The official requirement of strength in a pressure cabin called for a factor of safety of two; in other words the cabin must not fail if the normal working pressure of $8\frac{1}{4}$ lb., in the case of the Comet, was increased to $16\frac{1}{2}$ lb. per square inch. In designing we increased this factor of 2 to $2\frac{1}{2}$ so that the cabin would not fail until the pressure was more than 20 lb. to the square inch. It would be true to say that more *ought* to have been known about the conditions affecting fatigue, but apparently they were not known, or if known the knowledge was not made available. In our own cabin tests at Hatfield thousands of loadings had been applied without failure, but it was not enough because the conditions of fatigue had not been considered sufficiently as a dominant and vital factor.

Knowing the cause of the failures, together with the evidence from the wreckage, made it possible to visualize what had happened in the air. A fatigue crack had started and weakened the cabin structure so that it burst like a blown-up paper bag and was ripped to pieces in a fraction of a second. The passengers had been blown out and killed instantaneously, and the whole structure of the aircraft had broken up and disintegrated in a fraction of a second.

A Court of Inquiry was held on the Comet disasters and sat in Church House, Westminster between October 19, and November 24, 1954. The Rt. Hon. Lord Cohen was appointed to act as Commissioner with Sir William Farren, Professor W. J. Duncan and Air Commodore A. H. Wheeler as Assessors. The findings of the Court have been previously published in full. They dealt with the construction and testing of the Comet very thoroughly and are of considerable length. I am therefore taking typical statements from the findings which refer to the pressure cabin in particular, that being the source of the trouble.

In referring to our own cabin tests the report says:

'Throughout the design de Havillands relied on well-established methods essentially the same as those in general use by aircraft designers. But they were going outside the range of previous experience and they decided to make thorough tests of every part of the cabin structure.'

Again:

'de Havillands used a design pressure of $2\frac{1}{2}P$ ($2\frac{1}{2}$ times the working pressure) and tested the cabin to $2P$. . . . Their reasons for adopting these substantially higher figures were two. They believed, and this belief was shared by the Air Registration Board and other expert opinion, that a cabin that would survive undamaged a test to double its working pressure, $2P$, would not fail in service under the action of fatigue. . . .'

184

The Comet and After

In spite of the findings of the Court of Inquiry and the admittedly insufficient knowledge of fatigue problems, we realized that our technical reputation had suffered a reverse, and we also realized that it would take several years of hard work to regain our position. Those of our staff responsible for finance, business, sales and factory organization had the unenviable task of keeping things going during the long period of investigation and re-design.

We had made an unusually big advance in design instead of the more usual method of advancing on the built-up experience from preceding designs. Was the design and construction of the Comet justified? Under the circumstances I think it was. Someone was going to make a jet liner sometime, and although we suffered disaster, it caused attention to be focused, not only on pressure cabin design, but on the whole subject of metal fatigue. It accelerated research in this country and throughout the world and thus brought about greater knowledge of the problem.

There is little doubt that many previous aircraft accidents, civil and military, both here and abroad, were due to 'fatigue' in some critical part of the structure, but were written off as due to 'pilot's error' or 'cause of failure unknown'. Fatigue is obviously connected with strength. Excess strength means excess weight and less 'payload' carried. It is necessary to carry the maximum number of passengers (payload) to make air travel financially possible; it is obviously necessary also to have adequate strength of structure. One of the essentials of good design is a successful compromise in satisfying these conflicting demands of low weight and adequate strength.

There is no denying that we had been through a long period of what might be called 'technical depression' during which difficulties loomed greater than they really were. Uncertainty and waiting can be mentally devastating. We had repeatedly to remind ourselves that in the past thirty-five years we had made far more successful aircraft than failures, and there was no reason why we should not do so again. Now, with a clear picture of future requirements there was a gradual return of confidence in our own technical ability, and as the design of Comet 4 progressed this confidence grew into the faith and enthusiasm that overcomes all difficulties.

The Air Ministry helped us in every way possible. They took over some of the Comets for the various tests made at Farnborough, and others, with the necessary cabin modifications, were made available to Transport Command. Comets had been supplied to Air France and U.A.T., and they had been operated with great success and no failures, but they naturally had to be withdrawn from service. Two Comets of the Royal Canadian Air Force were eventually flown to England and the cabins were modified. They were flown back to Canada and one of them was used by H.M. the Queen and H.R.H. the Duke of Edinburgh during their visit in 1959.

The cabin modification to existing Comets was no small matter. It consisted chiefly of replacing the whole length of the window panel with one of much increased strength with special reinforcements round all 'cut outs', windows, hatches, doors and any other opening. With these alterations the safe life of the cabin structure was over ten thousand hours.

B.O.A.C. showed their continued faith in the jet liner by ordering twenty Comet 4s. There were certain new requirements, one of the most important being a safe life of thirty thousand hours. This meant that all major components would have to be tested to about five times this value. This was an unprecedented figure, but it was being forcibly realized that a modern airliner costing one million pounds, or more, must have a long life if it is to be a reasonably economical proposition.

We decided that it was essential to have the most up-to-date equipment for testing cabins under pressure. This meant a water tank large enough to take a complete fuselage and also equipment including the pumping gear and recording instruments as well as mechanism for putting alternating loads on the wings so that wing stresses that were transmitted to the fuselage were fully representative in the tests. Armed with all the experience we had gained from the numerous laboratory tests and the twenty-seven million miles of Comet flying, it was a relatively straightforward matter to turn this knowledge into sound engineering practice in the re-design of the Comet 3 into the Comet 4. Concentrated effort was made to produce the first new fuselage sections, and three full-scale specimens were produced representing the nose section, the centre section and the rear portion of the fuselage. These sections were each subjected to 120,000 reversals of pressure without failure, which is equivalent to 480,000 flying hours. In addition full-scale specimens of the wing spars and root joints were tested and all gave lives in excess of 180,000 hours. This same treatment was, of course, given to all major parts of the structure.

Finally, the aircraft was assembled and placed in the water tank and testing commenced on June 15, 1958. A representative four-hour flight was completed every two minutes and consisted of the applications to the wing and fuselage of all the average stresses occurring in actual flight, including wind gusts, landing stresses and, of course, cabin pressure build-up. This test was taken to the equivalent of 120,000 flying hours without failure.

Aubrey Burke (now Sir Aubrey), who had been Managing Director of our Engine Company for eleven years, had been Managing Director of The de Havilland Aircraft Company since 1956 and had done a lot of reorganization, especially on the production of the Comet 4, the good results of which were shown in the high quality of work and the speed-up in production. In America, Boeing,

Douglas and Convair were all busy making their first jet liners, and as delivery dates got nearer it looked as if Boeing might win the race for first place in a jet service across the Atlantic. In the case of the first Comet 4, a lot of people, and especially B.O.A.C., had a pleasant surprise when told that delivery would be as specified, but few people knew that their surprise was to be greater still when it was known that not one but *two* Comets would be delivered on the great day (and a third Comet four days later). It actually happened at London Airport on September 30, 1958. There was a handing-over ceremony with some speeches and champagne. The Comet 4 had started its career as the first jet liner in service across the Atlantic, a career that we hoped and believed would be long and successful. We had beaten our Boeing friends by a small margin. I don't think many of us felt like waving flags or talking about the phoenix rising from the ashes; it was more a feeling of profound relief and satisfaction.

When the Comet 4 had made the first regular passenger service crossing of the Atlantic we were greatly heartened when I received a telegram from Mr. Harold Macmillan, the Prime Minister. It read:

'Heartiest congratulations to you on your magnificent effort in getting the Comet 4 first off the mark in regular passenger service across the Atlantic. The resurgence of the Comet airliner is a fitting reward for the faith in the future of this fine product and the whole nation takes pride in the fact that a British aircraft has led the world into the new turbo-jet age.

Harold Macmillan.'

After the Comet 4 had been on the Atlantic service for a short time we were immensely pleased to receive from America the Elmer A. Sperry Award—'. . . for the vision, courage, and skills displayed in conceiving, developing and producing the world's first jet-powered passenger transport aircraft, the de Havilland Comet, powered by de Havilland "Ghost" jet engines. This accomplishment is especially noteworthy as providing the example and inspiration which has brought into being the succession of efficient, high-performance, subsonic jet transports that have followed under various leaderships throughout the world. . . .'

This was indeed a high honour and a generous gesture, and we valued it all the more as coming from our competitors who had contributed so much to the development of air transport.

We were also most gratified to receive, together with Rolls-Royce and B.O.A.C., the Hulton Achievement Award for 1959 which is presented annually '. . . to the individual or group making the most significant contribution to the prestige of the United Kingdom at home or abroad, and in industry, science, medicine, the arts or literature. . . .'

It also gave us great pleasure to receive the Viva Shield and Gold Medal from the Worshipful Company of Carmen for the production of the Comet.

There are some interesting sidelights on the Comet 1 accidents. Disasters have previously happened to British as well as foreign airliners. Some have disappeared without trace, but none has had world-wide publicity as intense and for so long as the Comet. I think this was because it was the first jet airliner, and something very new and successful that had caught public attention and imagination. The shock was all the greater when this was turned to tragedy.

When an air accident is clearly due to pilot's misjudgement it is usually described as due to human error, but surely all accidents—or anyhow 99 per cent—are due to human error. The error may originate in any one of the many departments involved: in the design of a detail part, in wrong stressing assumptions, in the actual construction or in the handling of the finished article. I do not know of a proved case of an aircraft being badly damaged by lightning. I have been in an airliner cabin in a storm during a test flight when a vivid 'ball of fire' appeared in the forward part of the cabin, accompanied by an explosion like a gunshot being fired, but the only sign on the aircraft was a minute hole in the cockpit nose. Nothing was felt by anyone, it was merely spectacular. The human error in the case of the Comet was the general lack of deeper knowledge of the problem of metal fatigue.

As well as the hundreds of letters of sympathy and goodwill we received, there were over three thousand of a different type which showed a wonderfully varied cross-section of thought and intention of the writers. These letters ranged from those genuinely wishing to give good advice to those of abuse and others demanding large sums of money for 'secret' information that would lead to the cause of the accidents. The writers putting forward reasons for the crashes rather naturally suggested something very unusual. There were several who thought the fumes of Vesuvius and Stromboli had affected the engines of the Comets. I had many letters that merely asked for money for no specific reason. Many writers claimed to know who had placed a bomb in the aircraft. All letters of this nature were handed to M.I.5 for their investigation, but produced nothing of importance.

Many well-meaning people suggested that the name COMET should be changed. I opposed this from the start. It seemed to me to be like a clumsy sort of cheating and would do more harm than good. It would be known sooner or later that we had deceived by a not very clever trick, and it was far better to prove that Comet failure was to be turned into Comet success.

During our investigations we were heartened and cheered by offers of help and co-operation from many of our competitors, including the American firms of Boeing and Douglas. Boeing sent three of their top technical staff to England and we had many interesting discussions and exchanges of ideas, but at the time of their visit the cause of the crashes was still a mystery, and Boeings were as mystified as we were.

There are now three types of the Comet 4, each with different range and seating capacity but similar in structure. All have given good service with the airline operators in various parts of the world, as well as with Transport Command of the Royal Air Force.

The development of airliners and our other types of smaller aircraft will continue indefinitely as new knowledge and experience is accumulated. There is no end in sight. Speeds will increase to figures that today seem fantastic. Comfort in air travel will surpass anything we now know. Wise people of the future will look back with interest and perhaps respect on our efforts as we look back now to the work of Cayley, Blériot and the Wright Brothers and many others as being links in the long chain of aeronautical progress.

CHAPTER THIRTEEN

FULL CIRCLE

I CAN now stand back and view the happenings of the past fifty years. There have been serious set-backs as well as many successes; there have been tragic personal losses, but risks of failure are inseparable from all new forms of progressive advance. Advance could not have come about without the very close co-operation and help of a great number of people working together, amongst whom are the many thousands in workshops and offices who have worked through bad times as well as good. The other directors of our firm and all its branches have carried the burden of financial and business matters successfully through difficult times. From the handful of people who started at Stag Lane forty years ago has grown a great enterprise which has lately amalgamated with another great enterprise—The Hawker-Siddeley Group. But this is not a coming together of strangers. In 1910 Tom Sopwith, having learnt to fly, was preparing his Howard Wright biplane to try for the Baron de Forest prize. This was to be awarded to the first pilot to fly the greatest distance from England to the Continent. I was also going to try for it if I could raise a few hundred pounds for expenses, but had still not succeeded when Sopwith set out and won the prize. Now, as Sir Thomas Sopwith, he is Chairman of the Hawker-Siddeley Group. I also knew Sir Roy Dobson in the early days. He is now Managing Director of the Group. Many of our people know many of their people and although amalgamations are sometimes 'difficult', I feel confident that in this case the result is going to be highly successful.

It is difficult to realize the immensity of the change in aeroplanes during the fifty years on which I, and those near my age, can look back. Earlier in this book I have told how my first aeroplane *including* engine, was built, crashed and rebuilt and flown for a cost of under £1,000. Admittedly it was very crude, but it did fly, and led on to steady development and improvement. Fifteen years later a really practical light 'plane, the Moth, was selling, new, for £650. Today our smallest practical light aeroplane sells at about five times this amount. The reasons for these great changes are many: higher wages, costly materials, greater complexity, the much lower value of money. All this is inevitable. But I think it would have been wise if the Government had done something to keep private flying more alive after the war. This neglect allowed America to build up a light 'plane industry that would be difficult or impossible to compete with.

My association with the works side of aircraft has been more and more limited since the early days at Stag Lane. This is largely due to the rapid increase in the number of men and women who do the actual work of making detail parts and assembling the complete machine. Whereas in the 1920s less than a hundred people built a light 'plane in a few months and one could know many of them well and see the work growing daily, today an airliner requires several thousand people working for two or three years to build it, and at times progress appears to be almost static. Under these conditions it becomes increasingly difficult to know any of the great number engaged on the work.

We have, with few exceptions, been free of labour troubles in almost all our factories, and I believe there exists a universally good spirit between management and workshop personnel. In this we are fortunate. I believe the seeds from which this spirit has grown were sown by Frank Hearle during his long term as Works Manager. He was on intimate terms with 'the shops', and was respected and liked. Affectionately known as 'Daddy Hearle', he would always listen to complaints and try to see the other man's point of view and take steps to remedy genuine complaints. The building of high quality machines such as aeroplanes must be of greater interest to those engaged on the work than in making, say, sanitary equipment, which has less glamour and is mass produced. Most motor-cars are also mass produced, although they are of high quality. But an aircraft is still largely a hand-made article and therefore means much more to those working on it.

Inevitably, there came a time when, due to age, I could no longer take an active part in design, and was asked to stay on as President of the Company, a position I still hold. The retired and semi-retired directors are able to meet at a small house in Hatfield overlooking the aerodrome, where we can deal with correspondence and have lunch. We are available, if and when called upon, to give an unofficial opinion on any subject that may come our way. Frank Hearle, Charles Walker (both retired) and I are the 'regulars' at the house, 'Highlands'. St. Barbe is becoming a more frequent visitor, while Nixon and other retired directors look in from time to time. Sometimes my correspondence is quite heavy and would create despair if I did not have an ideal secretary who not only deals with correspondence but acts as a most tactful 'keeper', constantly reminding me of appointments and a host of items I should otherwise overlook due to a failing memory. Ella Chapman has been my secretary for twenty-five years, and has been with the firm for twenty-six years. I cannot contemplate any sort of work without her help.

My interest in design matters remains, and I often invite members from the various technical departments, usually one at a time, to come to lunch and talk about their work. This is always of interest to me, and I like to think they benefit to some degree through being able to talk openly and freely about anything at all, work problems and also about their various hobbies and pastimes. This free and easy relationship is something for which I am deeply grateful. I have always found it natural to meet people on equal terms and treat them, and be treated, with complete freedom and sincerity. I am sure it is the only way in which to live and work in real harmony with others. This attitude grew up with us ever since the formation of the company in 1920, and it was helped by the fact that our total personnel was then less than a hundred and one knew most of them personally. By this system of informal discussions in a friendly and co-operative atmosphere the de Havilland Enterprise was built up over the years and now employs over 7,000 in workshops and offices.

Walker, Hearle and I do not attend the office every day unless there is something special on. One day I happened to say to Charles Walker that old age was an overrated pastime and that one got tired far too easily. He replied, typically: 'I quite agree, in fact I find it damn'd hard work just keeping alive.'

Hatfield is about fourteen miles from Stanmore where Hearle, Walker and I live fairly near each other. We all drive our own cars to 'Highlands'. I avoid main and arterial roads as far as possible, keeping to the pleasant country lanes. 'Highlands' is a quiet retreat well away from the racket of workshops and offices, but Hearle and I often go to see how work is progressing at the Aircraft factory, only half a mile away. One of the top designers usually acts as guide and gives us all the information that can be absorbed in a reasonable time. To inspect the modern airliner in detail would take days rather than hours, and the latest design of airliner, the D.H. Trident, is no exception. It is a three-engined 'plane with three

Rolls-Royce bypass jet engines clustered about the rear parts of the fuselage. Carrying 70–80 passengers and their luggage it will have a speed of 600 m.p.h. as compared with the Comet's 500. Twenty-four Tridents have been ordered by British European Airways who closely co-operated with us during the design stages. This airliner embodies all the improvements learned from Comet construction as well as from its operation in the hands of British Overseas Airways Corporation and other airlines. 'Pure' jet airliners seem to be coalescing into a roughly standard type; swept-back wings embodying large 'flaps' and leading edge slots and engines mounted on the rear of the fuselage. This position of the engines makes for less cabin noise and, more important, allows for a 'clean' wing uncluttered by engine mountings and air ducts, providing for a far better air flow and also giving much greater storage space for fuel. The first Trident is due to fly at the end of this year or early in the new year.

We are also building a small 6–8 executive 'plane with two engines at the rear. This 'plane will replace the 'Dove' of which over 500 have been built and are operating in most countries. But this new jet 'plane will cruise at 500 m.p.h. instead of the Dove's 180 to 200 m.p.h.

My interest in aeroplanes will always remain, but it is now more academic than active. Guided missiles and space travel would have been of far greater interest to me twenty or thirty years ago than they are today. There is almost no limit to the achievements in space travel, which may eventually be considered normal everyday happenings. Before that comes about, however, there must be the long period of trial and error and sacrifice, on a similar but far greater scale to that of the pioneering days of aviation. I have no desire whatever for the excitement of travelling to moon or planets. Let who will—and there will be a multitude—go in for space travel and I wish them well, but I am quite content to stay at home, as befits the old.

And what of my love for flying, now that I am in my eightieth year? My love for it has grown no less with the years, while the technical interest in testing aircraft, when I was still able to carry this out, was renewed with every new type I took up. I still love flying today, although I am afraid age and complying with regulations limit it to flying as a passenger. I am quite sure that the enjoyment I derived from flying, and the big number of hours I put in every year, added greatly to what ability I had as a designer. It gave me, for instance, invaluable first-hand knowledge of stability, control and general handling qualities of a number of different types. I think I should also say that in my flying career of forty-six years I had wonderfully good fortune. There have been many minor mishaps, several forced landings due to mechanical trouble or weather, but apart from the crash at Farnborough before the first war I have suffered no injury. This can certainly be put down in part at least to what is vaguely called 'luck', but it is also due to the fact that I had sufficient technical and aerodynamic knowledge to give me a very healthy respect for the real dangers of flying.

I was always well aware of the risk element in flying, and especially in test flying, and naturally gave this a lot of thought when my sons made this their career. In the early stages we often openly discussed the risks involved, especially compared with those in a ground or office job. Neither Geoffrey nor John took these talks very seriously. They started a strange habit of refusing to call aeroplanes by their proper name. Geoffrey usually referred to them as 'boilers'. 'If I take a boiler up and it blows up,' he used to say, 'it's just bad luck. But nothing's going to stop me.' John was usually even more terse, scarcely bothering to listen, and if he passed any comment at all it was certain to be an unseemly one, made with his always delightful smile.

Loneliness is hard to bear after many years of happy

197

married life, and I was feeling particularly lonely and miserable when, not long after Louie's death, I went out to Kenya. A safari with Colonel Stockley, a great authority on animals and butterflies, was a failure and we saw hardly any game. Then, on my return to Nyeri, feeling very depressed, I telephoned Joan Mordaunt, whom I had met two years before in Nairobi, and asked her to fix up a room in a hotel for me there. She did this with her usual efficiency, and when I met her she said, 'Why not go to Amboseli where you can be sure of seeing elephant, rhino, buffalo and lion as well as lots of smaller game.' I agreed that that was a good idea, and better still, suggested she came along with me. We flew down in a small 'plane and saw all the animals she had promised.

I soon became very fond of Joan, and when in 1951 she came to England to see her mother, who was 89 and very frail, I asked her to marry me. I bless the good fortune that gave me a second marriage that has been so happy and satisfactory. We have much in common, including an ardent love of nature and the country and most of the more peaceful pursuits, and a strong dislike of all ostentation and formal functions. Joan has a daughter, Ann, by her first marriage, and her son Philip is working in the drawing office at Hatfield. Her grandfather was W. Frith, R.A., famous for his picture of Derby Day now in the Tate Gallery, and Joan has recently proved the value of heredity in this art by taking up painting.

Now that I have much more time to myself I do not find that it in any way falls heavily on my hands. Photography still fascinates me although I do very little of it now. As a relaxation during the last war I started to build up a 'still' camera especially devised for taking big game, fast operation and easy handling being the main features. I had tried a Leica before the war but, while it was very handy, I thought it better to go for $2\frac{1}{4} \times 2\frac{1}{4}$ inch size of film so that originals could be 'blown up' to a really large size without loss of too much definition. Some of the results with this camera, used on big game in Africa, are included in this book. In recent years, though, I have done a certain amount of work with a cine-camera. My most ambitious project was the construction of a mechanism for operating this to take 'time lapse' coloured photographs of growing flowers and plants, and later to film the life history of the swallow tail butterfly, which was shown, but only in black-and-white of course, on Peter Scott's *Look* programme on television. For filming growing plants a time lapse of twenty or thirty minutes was necessary, for the opening of flowers three to five minutes was usual. The device often worked for three or four weeks, day and night, without attention, and when the film was projected the growth could be speeded up seven thousand times.

My reading is done mainly in bed at night and early morning. At night it is always Westerns, of which I have a small and precious collection, all of which I know almost by heart. There may not be any excitement of anticipation at the climax, but they never fail as peaceful escapism, in spite of the violence and killings. In the morning I turn to harder stuff—natural history, biographies, scientific journals, books on evolution, a subject which has always greatly interested me.

During the daytime, when not at Hatfield, I spend a fair amount of my time in my workshop, making and mending. Our house and garden are now rather too large, but the garden is a joy to Joan, who loves it and tends it with skill and care. It is also a joy to me, so long as I am allowed to do only the minimum possible work in it, and if possible none at all. Sometimes, though, I can be seen wheeling away a barrow of grass cuttings, and I have been known to make adjustments to the lawn mower for Joan.

Quite recently Joan and I went to Oxford to look at Medley again. We dreaded the shock we felt sure was in store for us. We had made the last visit many years ago, when it looked sadly derelict. But this time we were delighted to see that it was recovering from the years of neglect, and had every chance of becoming again the lovely secluded home it was when I was young. Considering that it is but three miles from the centre of Oxford, I had expected villas or blocks of flats to be growing all around it, but there is still no other building in sight and almost the whole estate has escaped spoliation. The reason for this is that the present owners bought the place freehold from the previous occupant with the intention of efficiently farming the 150 acres and renewing the charm of the house and grounds.

I had a few regrets, but they were easily outweighed by the feeling of pleasure and promise that was first aroused. The lily pond that had been my great joy when I was a boy, and where I had spent a vast amount of time in fishing for tench, roach and perch, is now choked with dead reeds and surrounded by weeds; but perhaps that will be altered in time. The house, covered with ivy for many years, is now bare and looks—probably only to me—a little naked, but at least reveals where repairs are necessary.

There used to be a great elm tree at the bottom of the garden only a few yards from the river margin. Seventy years ago I thought of the tree as the greatest in England, if not the world. For me there has always been a sort of mystic splendour about trees, especially trees of great size. Standing close to the trunk and looking up into the branches of that great tree used to give me a feeling of awe and wonder and a sense of great peace. But the great elm tree had gone, felled in order to save the destruction of the old garden wall only a few yards away.

But there is another great tree quite near the front of the house. It is a sycamore, and although of great age is still healthy and has fine foliage. Its gnarled and relatively short trunk must be five feet or more in diameter. My mother often told how she used to climb into the lower branches from a ladder when she was a little girl; and even then it had been a great tree.

The yard, still surrounded by workshops, carriage house, stables and cottage is, miraculously, hardly altered at all, and the forge of old Cox, the blacksmith of far-off days, has been put into full use again for the many odd jobs of repair and renewal on a big farm. This was a pleasing sign, and there was another one. When four or five years old I remember my mother making a full-sized drawing for a weathercock that actually represented a barnyard cock, complete with fine tail feathers and up-standing comb. This drawing was handed to Cox, who pasted it on sheet iron and cut out an iron weathercock; and there, on the highest roof ridge over the stable where it was fixed over seventy years ago, was the same weather-cock, still working. My mother had originally painted it in gay colours, red, black and white tail feathers and a bright red comb, but after seventy years there was little or no colour to be seen, which is hardly surprising. It seemed incredible that it could have lasted so long, but I was assured that it was, without any doubt, the original.

As we walked from the yard through the short passage into the garden and passed the potting shed, that precious scent of mustiness and damp earth greeted us, and recalled for me early memories and happy days.

It often happens that to go back to childhood haunts and times turns out to be sadly disappointing, for every-thing looks smaller and unfamiliar, shrunken in size as well as in appeal. In our visit to the old manor all this was reversed. There was nostalgia, perhaps, but this was over-ruled by excitement and pleasure as if coming home after a long and wearying journey. I could again see my grand-father, Jason Saunders, walking unhurriedly in the garden with his 'square' bowler hat, and spud walking stick, and I recalled how, while he was still living here, I had men-tioned the vague talk one heard from time to time about the possibility of man being able one day to imitate the birds and really fly. He would smile indulgently, but he never scoffed at the idea.

As I looked around me I knew that it was here that I had spent many of the happiest days of my life, it was here that the seed of my life's work was really germinated through the generosity, kindliness and understanding of a man of great character.

Now my work was done, and I was back to see, once again, the happy familiar scene.

CHAPTER FOURTEEN

AND SO INTO SPACE

Looking to the future of aeroplane travel, there are many problems, the outcome of which is difficult to forecast. What will be the ultimate speed? It will, of course, be supersonic, but having achieved much higher speeds, new and difficult problems arise. New heat-resisting construction will be needed. Landing and take-off may have to be modified from horizontal to vertical, and noise will be a major problem. Jet propulson will probably remain for a considerable time, but one day it is likely to be replaced by nuclear power. In the best modern jet air-liners there is limited scope for improvement in passenger comfort. Still better seats and more space are possible but I doubt if sleeping bunks will be required because at 2,000 miles an hour few journeys will take more than two or three hours. The passenger will not be conscious of the actual speed even if it was much above 2,000 miles per hour. Having attained full speed following a reasonable acceleration he will not *feel* any difference from travelling at 100 miles per hour.

But travelling at very high speeds will have little advan-tage until terminal delays are reduced to the minimum, The first delay is in getting to the departure airport. There are various ways of vastly reducing this delay. Helicopters might fly from a city centre, a monorail might be con-structed at great expense, but I feel strongly in favour of using a conventional type aeroplane but designed with a view to achieving very short take-off run, slow landing (these qualities usually go together), ample performance

203

on one engine and auto-landing. It should be a relatively easy 'plane to design; more than a germ of the idea is already embodied in the 'Caribou', designed by our Canadian company and which is in fairly large production for the United States Air Force and several other operators in many countries. The speed need not be great, 100 to 150 m.p.h. would beat any other form of transport for this particular purpose. The fuel carried need be relatively very light in weight because only a small amount would normally be needed, and the piloting would not require special skill. This type of 'plane could be adequately silenced. The take-off for such a plane could be from the roof of a large building like a railway station or from roofs linked up by a runway, a runway that would be very short compared with those used at a terminal airport.

The other delays, Customs, passports, luggage stowage and just sitting about waiting must be dealt with by the airline concerned. The aircraft constructor cannot help much.

Many different types of commercial aeroplane will be required, not only the very fast ones; freight-planes, small private or executive types, crop-spraying 'planes and those designed for short and medium distances. The propeller section of our company deals also with guided missiles and rocketry. As my knowledge of space travel is somewhat rudimentary I have asked Mr. Guy Gardiner, a leading director, to arrange for one of his space travel specialists, Mr. Geoffrey Pardoe, to give his views in the following pages. Most people are naturally amazed at the rapid developments of this new science, surely the most advanced that mankind has ever evolved, and with future possibilities staggering in their vast implications. There are several points of special significance in Mr. Pardoe's article. The Blue Streak rocket we were asked to build by the Government was the only rocket in Europe capable of putting a satellite into orbit, but when about fifty million pounds had been spent and the rocket was more than half finished, it was stopped. Why not at least have 'fired' a few of these rockets and gained valuable data instead of wasting fifty million pounds? His remarks on the commercial possibilities of the rocket are most significant and promising, and yet have limited chance of being developed. It is a sad story.

Within an hour of writing the above, news came in of the first man in space, Major Yuri Gagarin, launched by the Russians on April 12, 1961.

'AND SO INTO SPACE'

General Background

There is an interesting similarity in the world of aviation between the periods at the beginning of each half of this century; on the first occasion the challenge of airborne flight was being met—and was accompanied by a struggle to convince the sceptics that the new-found ability to fly would have a wide impact on the way of life in future years—even though in detail it could not be explained how this would be realized. Now we are taking the first few steps into space and so opening up a new era of exploration. The problem of visualizing the full impact of this on the future course of events, is just as difficult; it is unfortunate, however, that the similarity ends here, as we are not yet among the pioneers in these new adventures in Space.

The driving spirit to explore these new areas is strongly evident in scientists and engineers in this country, but the problems of space (and the vehicles to reach into it) are so massive, that the effort needed to produce and launch space vehicles can no longer be mounted by a single company, and indeed it would appear that it is beyond the means of most single countries to provide the necessary engineering and financial support. Unlike the pioneering days of aircraft, therefore, serious entry into space depends on extensive Government support. Decisions with regard to the extent that this country will participate in space programmes, have been slow to emerge from the British Government, and the situation has been further complicated by the proposed collaboration with European countries on the development of the launching vehicles.

The Blue Streak Project

We at Hatfield are involved in Space to a major degree, by virtue of our work on Blue Streak, *which is the only European rocket of suitable size to act as the first propulsion stage (or booster) for a multi-stage Space vehicle.*

Following our entry into the guided weapon field in 1951, we became involved with large ballistic rockets in 1955 when the contract was placed with the de Havilland Propeller Company to act as prime contractors for the design and development of the Blue Streak ballistic missile; the Propeller Company had the responsibility of co-ordinating the activities of other contractors, namely the de Havilland Aircraft Company for the structure, Rolls-Royce Limited for the rocket engines, Sperry Gyroscope Company for the inertial guidance system—and in the early days Marconi's and English Electric for alternative guidance system. De Havilland's were also responsible for the systems engineering and the integration of the design, and subsequent assembly, of equipment, supplied from the other contractors, into the overall weapon. De Havilland's were also to design the re-entry head, and conduct the flight trials on the weapon in Australia, in conjunction with both British and Australian Government establishments.

In Australia we established a large team of engineers to work in collaboration with the Australian Weapons Research Establishment at Woomera, both to prepare the launching pads and associated facilities ready for the Blue Streak trials, and later to support the trials work in conjunction with the teams sent out from England with each missile.

And So Into Space

By the time of the cancellation of Blue Streak as a military weapon in April 1960, the de Havilland Propeller and Aircraft Companies had together built up a team of several thousand highly skilled engineers, employed at various test sites and factories throughout England and Australia: they covered an exceptionally wide part of the spectrum of engineering skills—at one extreme, large civil and mechanical engineering structures for handling, transporting and launching the rockets, whilst at the other extreme, high precision electronic and mechanical engineering, associated with the components of the systems of the rocket. By 1960 several partially equipped rocket vehicles had been produced, and were under test at our test site at Hatfield, at the Spadeadam Rocket Establishment, Cumberland (jointly used by Rolls-Royce Limited and de Havilland Propellers), and one rocket had actually been sent in parts, by sea and air, to Australia, for early development work at the Woomera range.

From Ballistic Missiles to Space Rockets

In the same way that the first generation of American Space Rockets was largely evolved from the use of military ballistic missiles (such as Thor and Atlas), so is Blue Streak suitable as the first stage of a space rocket. In the year following the cancellation of the military weapon, development of the appropriate parts of Blue Streak as a space vehicle was continued at a slower tempo, pending a decision to enter into a full scale programme.

From 1959 onwards our engineers had been considering ways in which Blue Streak could be used for the exploitation of space. The first of these ideas was published in 1959 at the Commonwealth Space Flight Symposium, and subsequently proposals for both civil and military uses of Blue Streak as a space rocket have been progressively expanded.

During 1960 de Havilland engineers at the Canadian company were already engaged in designing and fabricating the structure of a satellite known as S51 which the Canadian Government were arranging to launch into orbit with an American rocket. This joint American/Canadian project is known as the Canadian Top Side experiment, and it is designed to measure amongst other things, those features of the ionosphere which are of direct interest to Canada. In addition to their work in producing the actual structure of the satellite, the Canadian engineers in the Special Products Division have developed an ingenious method of providing extensible radio aerials in the satellite. Not only will this device be used in Canadian satellite tests, but it has also been adopted for other American satellites. So quite apart from the experience acquired over the last few years in England, our organization has already started to acquire experience in the manufacture of equipment for the orbital environment.

First Steps towards New Horizons

Of the various types of missions envisaged within our present limited knowledge of the potential of space-flight, there is no doubt that experiments designed for scientific research beyond the atmosphere of earth, and out into the solar system, will continue indefinitely. The field of exploration is unlimited, and although the new information already gained about our universe is extensive, we are but scratching the surface of the depths of space. Most of the space research experiments so far carried out have been with equipment installed in satellites and space probes whose size is of the order of only a few hundreds of pounds of mass—some only tens of pounds or less; in spite of this many major new facts have been discovered relating to cosmic radiation characteristics, micro-meteorite intensity, magnetic fields, etc., to name but a few. Most of the work so far has been limited to within a few thousand miles of the surface of the Earth—even the moon (at a quarter of a million miles away from the Earth) is within the inner fringes of outer space; for example, light travelling at 186,000 miles per second takes just over one second to reach the moon from the earth, whereas this light would take over 8 minutes to our sun, over 4 years to our nearest star, and over one million years to our nearest galaxy! Even if we could project space craft at speeds approaching that of the speed of light (which is an extremely optimistic suggestion), then on a time basis we are clearly limited to exploration within our own solar system for many decades to come—until, in fact, some new interpretation of the laws of nature enables us to harness energy for transportation of matter in ways beyond our present imagination.

Against this background of the immensity of space, however, we should keep clearly in view the impressive reality of space activity as it is already today. More than fifty satellites have been sent up into orbit around our earth, space probes have circled the moon and photographed its far side, other probes have been sent out into the solar system and one in particular has been sent to the near vicinity of Venus and contact has been established with man-made equipment from distances across Space of many tens of millions of miles; a variety of animals have been established in orbit around the earth and successfully brought back through the atmosphere to a safe landing and successful survival. Not only animals but important recording equipment has been recovered from space and, in the Discoverer series of American experiments, capsules brought down from orbit have been snatched by aircraft whilst descending by parachute in the final phase of the re-entry. Voices, music and pictures have been successfully bounced off the Moon from continent to continent, and the American Navy uses this means of transmission as a regular feature between its Maryland base in America and its Hawaii Naval Station. 100 ft. diameter balloons have been launched over the surface of the Earth. The recorded voice of the last President of America has been carried into orbit and retransmitted to the ground via a communication satellite, and other forms of communication satellites have already received and transmitted information to and from the Earth when in orbit. A multitude of television pictures have been taken by both infra-red and optical cameras, mounted in satellites for the purpose of developing systems to give early warning of ballistic missiles—and (on a more peaceful scale) to examine the world's weather in order to improve meteorological services. Satellites with cameras have already been launched to reconnoitre enemy territory. So much data has been produced by space experiments to date that many of the tests have been slowed down in order that methods may be developed to analyse and distribute the data pouring in from Space.

Commercial Exploitation of Space

Work is already directed towards the commercial use of space, where high financial dividends can be expected from investments which are of a comparable order with many industrial developments. There is no doubt whatsoever that the first use of space that will be of direct value to the general public will be that of long distance international communication by earth satellites. In America, work is far advanced, by several leading companies, on equipment which will enable patterns of satellites to be projected into orbit around the earth, each satellite carrying radio receiving and transmitting equipment, to relay telephone and television signals from one ground station back to another and so encompassing the world.

Present means of communication by cable and by radio links have many limitations; submarine cables are very costly to lay (some £90 million is anticipated for a round-the-world cable linking existing ground circuits) and they are limited by the physical size of the cable to carry only some tens of channels of conversation. Such a system, therefore, gives only limited service to many parts of the world. Radio contact around the globe at present depends on signals being reflected by the ionized layers a few hundred miles above the surface of the earth—and this service is frequently interrupted by electrical disturbances to these ionized layers. Communication satellites make use of radio frequencies which are far higher than those at present used for such communications, and by their very nature they are independent of any disturbances to the ionized layers through which they pass. Not only, therefore, does a communication satellite system offer improved quality and more reliability than at present, but also it is capable of being used for normal television transmission which is impossible over very long distances by cable, due to technical limitations and the large number of amplifying stations needed along the cable. Whilst we in this country are several years away from when we may hope to use our own rockets to launch such satellites, engineers from our Company have made proposals for such communication systems, based on Blue Streak, and their studies of the economics of such an endeavour demonstrate forcibly that, from a reasonably modest system, large financial rewards can be obtained—£500 million accumulating over the first twenty years of operation is the order of profit, and this is associated with pessimistic figures for the cost of establishing and operating such a system.

One of the earlier systems that our engineers had in mind was a pattern of eight satellites, each of a few hundred pounds in weight and providing several hundreds of channels of telephone conversations (and possibly a television link) integrated with a pattern of twenty-four ground stations situated at strategic points around the world, thus serving both Commonwealth and other countries.

Another commercial use of space which has been receiving our considerable attention is that of navigation of ships (and later aircraft) using satellites as radio beacons;

these satellites would be observed by tracking equipment located in the ship and the output from an associated computer on the ship would provide information on position and course to a far greater degree of accuracy than can be obtained with present equipment and in all weather conditions.

Early prototypes of both communication and navigation satellites have already been fired by the Americans in their rockets, and the feasibility of such work is already established. It is with this in mind that it is worth repeating again that the use of space is already good business, and is attracting serious consideration by industrialists; the present state is far removed from the fictional haze which surrounded the concept of space flight until very few years ago.

With regret space is already becoming an arena of military activity; in many ways this is not surprising when one recalls that every other medium of travel on, below or above the surface of earth has been exploited for military use immediately the means have become available for man or his equipment to enter the new areas. So it is with space; already prototypes of military reconnaissance satellites are circling the earth, and whilst any future combat in space may be far removed from present conceptions of war, there is no doubt that work at present under way to develop satellites will lead to both passive and active military use. In the last category, satellites are being developed which will investigate and intercept other satellites; all of these functions will generate a vital military importance to space flights.

Man in Space

High on the list of priorities in American and Russian space work at present is that of developing rockets and satellites to take a man into space and return him safely to earth. 1961 will almost certainly be the vital year[1] when

[1] Written before the recent successful Russian and American space flights.

a man is first released from the bonds of gravity if only for a few quick circuits of the earth. The stimulus of adventure, and the enormous prestige which will result from the first successful attempt, have undoubtedly acted as a tremendous incentive to the two contesting nations for this prize. The cold logical reasons for wanting to do this are, at present, somewhat less clear; man's ability to discriminate (in comparison with electronic equipment) is sometimes offered as a good reason for developing the means of sending him into space, and yet this point is contested strongly by experts in computer techniques, who contend that adequate discrimination could be built into computers.

A more likely reason that has been suggested for having a man in space, is for the role of 'servicing engineer' to inspect and rectify complicated electronic equipment which may have been placed into orbit for the purpose of communication, navigation or military reconnaissance, etc. Orbital rendezvous techniques which would have to be used by space rockets to achieve this, are being worked on in some detail now; the analysis of the logistics of using such rendezvous vehicles, compared with the repair by replacement method, will qualify the urgency for developing man-carrying space vehicles. This early work on manned space flight is best considered as an insurance against a sudden fundamental need for such capability. It is within the performance of a Blue Streak multi-stage rocket to put a manned capsule into orbit a few hundred miles above Earth (say a 2,000-lb. capsule at 300 miles above the Earth). However, for the reasons discussed, no proposals are being put forward at present for this, as we may anticipate achieving our objectives in space for many years to come, with automatic equipment not dependent on manned operations.

New Techniques for Space Vehicle Development

The comparison between the problems of development and testing a large ballistic rocket, and those problems concerned with developing an aircraft, reveals some of the new techniques which have been introduced in our company in all phases of the work. To start with, the rocket test problems are accentuated by the fact that each vehicle must be expendable and yet each is in the same order of cost as a medium-sized jet airliner. Moreover, the phase of powered and controlled flight of a space vehicle is only a few minutes' duration, and yet all measurements of the flight must be made and transmitted to the ground in this time. The overwhelming advantage of the hours of testing available with even a single prototype aircraft is obvious by comparison. During this vehicle testing period means must be provided for the vehicle to be destroyed should it go wrong (since accidental impact with the ground could obviously cause severe damage) and so there is an added risk that, as a result of a minor failure (which could be accepted in a manned aircraft) the whole test may be invalidated in the case of a Space Vehicle. A large rocket development programme may amount to only ten launches; for the booster stage alone there would be, at the most, about three minutes of controlled flight per launch—which would give an aggregate of about thirty minutes of flight testing, during which time the technical integrity and reliability of the whole system must be demonstrated. Clearly this problem requires a completely different method of solution to that of an aircraft; the missile problem carries the attendant stimulus to develop high reliability and fully-automatic monitoring and recording techniques.

The propellants of a typical ballistic missile are liquid oxygen and kerosene and when these are mixed together in certain circumstances they form a highly explosive mixture; therefore when the missile is fuelled, all final testing must be conducted remotely and from protected positions, requiring remotely controlled electronic equipment. It can be seen, therefore, that a strong electronic engineering department is a fundamental part of a space rocket design team and the electronic work must be integrated most carefully with the structural and propulsion work.

A single rocket engine for a space booster develops a thrust of 60 to 70 tons and this in itself has meant the construction of very large and strong test rigs. These, for Blue Streak, are located at the Rocket Propulsion Establishment, Westcott, and at Spadeadam in Cumberland. At the latter place there are three complete engine rigs and three further stands can take complete Blue Streaks to test all systems, including engine firings. In all these static test facilities systems must be checked and double checked, not only to produce the right performance but also an adequate reliability to ensure maximum chance of a successful launch subsequently in Australia.

Of all the American attempts to place satellites into orbit, nearly half have been successful. Generally, therefore, two or three launches must be scheduled in a flight development programme, for every one successful test. There are, of course, exceptions to this general trend, and one of them, happily, is the British Black Knight test vehicle; the first nine attempts to launch this rocket were all successful, which is a remarkable achievement, and gives great confidence in the British approach to large rocket development.

Not only does the nature of a space vehicle require the introduction of these new techniques and facilities, to evolve performance and reliability, but the creation of such testing facilities adds considerable cost and time to the programme. To some degree the tests on various systems and missiles must be sequential, and with the comparatively few missiles available in the programme, several months may occur between firings. Moreover, if a particular launch is unsuccessful this can introduce a lengthy

215

gap in time between successful tests, all of which increases the managerial problem of maintaining a steady work load on the various divisions of the organization. Our Management Staff therefore has been carefully selected to ensure that their background enables them to expand their outlook to deal with these many new and varied problems which have been superimposed on tasks normally encountered within an aircraft company. In the case of Blue Streak a particular problem arises since the bulk of the rocket equipment is made in the Midlands and the South of England; the complete rocket is statically tested in the North of England, and must then be shipped to Australia for subsequent launching from Woomera. The transport problem alone injects many months into the programme, between assembly of the rocket, and the time it is launched into space.

With the missile the risk factor is greater, and of a different nature, than with the aircraft. As mentioned previously a missile spends a significantly large part of its testing time in a potentially explosive condition. The faulty operation of a disturbingly large number of individual components can cause complete loss of a vehicle both during test or flight. In test, the time of flight is short and the chance of in-flight rectification is effectively zero— unless everything works, then all is lost.

These problems are clearly not limited to the research and development phase of a space vehicle, but the reliability and servicing problem must be met, and overcome, when in operation. 'Operation' itself has a different meaning, as each multi-stage rocket is used only once and for only a few minutes at that. A satellite which goes wrong after being placed in orbit must be replaced by another being fired; although this situation can be improved to some extent by including in the satellite spare components which can be switched in to take the place of those which may have failed. Again there is the possibility (in the somewhat distant future) of repairs being carried out by a man in orbit.

And So Into Space

The Future

At the beginning of this note, an analogy was made between the present situation in space, and the beginning of the era of manned flight in the atmosphere. With this in mind one must accept that the present methods used in rockets to conquer space are crude and costly in comparison with techniques which will be commonplace in fifty years' time. One obvious area in which this will become apparent is that of propulsion; at the moment high thrusts are achieved by chemical means—burning liquids to produce hot gases. Already improved techniques are being developed—such as hot gases derived by nuclear means, rather than chemical, and by direct use of electrical energy to produce very low rocket thrusts. It is known already that chemical rockets have upper limits of efficiency, and indeed the monster rockets being planned for use in the latter part of this decade may well be among the largest physical size of rockets ever produced. They must surely be superseded by rockets of similar mass but of infinitely greater energy potential. The most probable area of propulsion advancement is in the electro-nuclear field, and it is of interest that magnetic fields, electrically generated in satellites, are already being used to adjust their attitude by interaction with the Earth's magnetic field. We may well see developments of these principles, leading to new sources of motive power at present inconceivable.

By the trends already evident, we may expect the aircraft industry to expand in diverse ways to meet the challenge of space, and at the same time continue to evolve new generations of military and civil aircraft to use the atmosphere with increasing effect. Space rockets and aircraft should not be considered as separate entities, as in some respects their operation, and the stimulus created by their design, will be complementary features in the challenging world of aviation.

THE following are extracts from the reports on
Mosquito aircraft during the last war compiled by my
brother, Hereward de Havilland.

December 1941

'The first operational unit to receive Mosquitoes was
No. 1 P.R.U. (Photo Reconnaissance) at Benson under
Wing Commander Geoffrey Tuttle. The 'plane was
accepted by all flying personnel as being something quite
outstanding; in my experience it is one of the only aircraft
which, initially, has not been branded by pilots as a death
trap in one way or another. On the other hand, the engineering and maintenance personnel, especially the
younger generation, were definitely biased against it,
mainly on account of wood construction.'

'Initial night flying has brought to notice several points
that need attention. They should be dealt with promptly
and embodied in future aircraft.'

March 1942

'The Mosquito, in a few months, has achieved a popu-
larity which I should think must be almost unique, in that
its praises are sung not only by pilots but *also by maintenance staffs*, and although there are quite a few legitimate
grouses . . . Owing to our obviously unfulfillable original
delivery dates we have come in for some severe criticism,
because A.O.C.s aren't interested in planning for production but in planning for action.'

'The question of pressure cabins came up, and as an
example of what can happen, it was said that an "expert"

bomb aimer with the latest bomb sight had dropped two bombs from 34,000 feet on Bremen (not from a Mosquito). Bomb aimer and members of the crew reported that the first was a direct hit and the second a "near miss". Less than four hours later P.R.U. photographed the area. The nearest bombs were *six and a half miles from the target.* After this high altitude bombing without pressure cabins is not considered very worthwhile.'

April 1942

'The cowling and exhaust manifold defects are the most serious ones yet encountered on the Mosquito. Most of their machines being unserviceable, it was decided to give some of the officers a party at Hatfield. The D.H. team beat them at squash. Later the Mosquito was "re-designed" over a fairly fluid dinner at the Comet, and Hopgood, who is Slade's radio operator during the war and a barrister in peacetime, talked dreamily of sex, exhaust manifolds and his dislike of Gandhi during the drive back to my cottage, where he slept soundly.'

May 1942

'A Mosquito contacted a Heinkel 111 and opened fire with cannon. The Heinkel returned the fire, putting bullets through both starboard main spars and aileron, both tail plane spars, port elevator, port airscrew dome and engine main glycol pipe. The Mosquito closed to eight yards and fired shells. The Heinkel's port engine caught fire and it did a slow spiral into the sea. The pilot of the Mosquito feathered one airscrew and flew back 140 miles on one engine.'

'On May 31st, the day after the 1,000-bomber night raid on Cologne, Mosquito bombers went into action for the first time. Cologne was the target, and four aircraft left at short intervals, starting at 5.30 a.m. They each carried two 250-lb. and two 500-lb. bombs, and went over at 24,000 feet. On arrival they found a towering column of smoke, reaching up to 14,000 feet, which obliterated Cologne entirely, but they dropped their bombs for luck. No flak and no fighters.

Two more went out at 11.45, high level, and Sqd. Ldr. Channer left to try and get low level photographs in the evening. He crossed the coast as low as possible, and after a time the cloud level came down to 1,000 feet. He went up into this for a time and when about sixty miles from Cologne opened up to +6 lb. boost and shallow-dived to very near the ground at 380 m.p.h. indicated. He noticed that when passing over a large marshalling yard, nobody looked up at him. Cattle in fields took no notice until he was well past them.

He told me afterwards that this flight impressed him more than any he had ever done before, and greatly strengthened his belief in the soundness of low Mosquito attacks on selected targets.'

June 1942

'The leakage of water into the cockpit during flight has already been reported to the Design Office, and an effort must be made without delay to remedy this. Apart from being thoroughly "putting off" for pilots during combat in particular, it will lead to all sorts of electrical and A.I. troubles and has already necessitated the dismantling of switchbox B and the changing of switches. I wish to emphasize the importance of this point which will, of course, increase during the winter months.'

'Embry's request to convert eight of his night fighters into intruders has been turned down, anyway for the present. In his letter to Slessor he wrote: "In my opinion the Mosquito is the finest aeroplane, without exception, that has ever been built in this country."'

Appendix I

'Of the second formation, one turned back after losing the other two in low cloud. These two, with Hughes leading, and Sgt. Rowlands on his left, got within twenty miles of the target when Rowlands felt a slight jar and his observer found pieces of chimney pot in his lap and a large hole in the fuselage side. The port engine started to vibrate rather badly and was closed down to 2,300 r.p.m. Rowlands couldn't keep up with Hughes owing to the port engine, so found a town, dropped his bombs on it, and turned for home. After getting well clear of the enemy coast he feathered the port propeller and landed at Norwich without further incident. The condition of the aircraft and port spinner is shown in an attached photograph.'

'On July 8th, Flying Officer Bayley of P.R.U. Leuchars, set out to find and photograph the battleship *Tirpitz* which was known to be somewhere well north of Narvik. Arrangements had been made for him to land at Murmansk and operate from there until the job was completed.

He found the *Tirpitz* and photographed her on his way there, landed, refuelled and returned to Leuchars, thus covering 3,000 miles during one day. He told me that Murmansk has been heavily bombed recently and the town is in ruins: the dock appears to have suffered less damage so far.'

'*Cockpit waterproofing and ventilation.* This has been complained of time after time. *Can something please be done.*'

September 1942

'The average life of aircraft of No. 105 (Bomber) Squadron up to the time they were either totally destroyed or reported missing during July, August and September 1942, was 67, 55 and 65 hours respectively.'

Appendix I

'*Summary up to September 30th,* 1942:

Mosquito aircraft missing	28
Mosquito aircraft totally destroyed	16
	44
Mosquito aircraft damaged, category AC	29
Mosquito aircraft damaged, category B	12
Fatal flying accidents	4
Enemy aircraft destroyed	20
Enemy aircraft probably destroyed	7
Enemy aircraft damaged	6
Weight of bombs dropped	112 tons'

'*September 25th*:

Four Mosquitoes set out from Leuchars to bomb Gestapo headquarters in Oslo from low altitude. The formation was originally to have been led by Wing Commander Edwards, but this arrangement was altered at the last minute by Bomber Command, and Sqd. Ldr. Parry took Edwards' place. They attacked in two pairs, Parry leading the first pair, with P/O Rowlands close up on his starboard quarter; then came F/O Bristow, with Sgt. Carter on his right. During the run up to the target, three F.W.190s made a diving attack from the starboard quarter, one going for the leading pair and two for the second. Bristow had to turn a few degrees left to get on to his target, and Carter on LK.325 was thus left rather farther astern and was hit; one of Rowlands' airscrews was hit by a cannon shell which exploded on the spinner.

Parry's aiming was good, and Rowlands actually saw his bombs strike the roof of the Gestapo building. After being hit, Carter turned left, and was last seen, still under control, making towards Sweden with one engine apparently on fire and a fighter on his tail.'

'*Exhaust System*. Exhaust manifolds are still by far the greatest source of trouble. As mentioned in the last

222

bulletin, several manifolds have been repaired repeatedly, and although the majority of aircraft are now fitted with the additional cooler ducts, it is not possible to judge their effectiveness unless new manifolds also have been fitted. It can be said, however, that the cooler ducts have materially increased the life of the manifolds; at least one aircraft has completed over 100 hours without troubles, and several have completed over fifty hours.'

'*Cockpit ventilation.* After months of complaints, a very simple and effective cure for excessive cockpit heat has at last been produced, consisting of a suction louvre in the detachable inspection panel and top of the wing.

January 1943

'On January 27th (1943) W/C John Cunningham took over 85 Squadron from Raphael, who is going to Canada for a month, prior to becoming Station Commander at Castle Camps.'

'*Nos.* 105 *and* 139 *Squadrons, Marham*

These squadrons have made a large number of sorties at dawn, during daylight, at dusk and some at night. There is now a strong feeling of discontent on the station because aircraft already allotted to 139 to bring this unit up to strength have been transferred en bloc to No. 109 Pathfinder Squadron, and it seems doubtful whether Marham will get their quota of reinforcements, which they badly need now if they are to carry on.

Both these Squadrons, particularly 105, have now done a considerable amount of "ground level" bombing—probably more than any other R.A.F. unit—and their crews are so used to the technique that the percentage of bombs which actually go inside the building aimed for is now large. Although the Fortress high level bombing is, at times, extremely accurate, they do not claim to be able to put bombs *inside*, say, a small factory target, unless 50 tons or so are dropped, and it has yet to be shown whether they can operate efficiently on targets well inside Germany.'

'On Saturday, January 30th, the tenth anniversary of Hitler's régime, Mosquitoes bombed Berlin twice in daylight. The time of arrival of the first raid was arranged to coincide with the opening of Goering's speech at 11.0 a.m. Three Mosquitoes of 105 Squadron took part, DZ.413, DZ.372 and DZ.408, and all arrived on time. They flew low as far as the enemy coast, to fox the R.D.F., then climbed to 25,000 ft., bombed from 20,000, and came home in a steady power descent from that height. There was very little opposition of any sort at Berlin, but Reynolds got very intense and accurate flak over Bremen on the way back at 20,000 feet. Times (not including warming up and taxiing) and consumptions were as follows: DZ.413—412 gallons in 4 hrs. 36 mins., DZ.372—450 gallons in 4 hrs. 42 mins., DZ.408—450 gallons in 5 hrs. 03 mins. The total track mileage was 1,145.

The afternoon raid consisted of two aircraft of 105 Squadron and one of 139 (Sqd. Ldr. Darling). They were due to arrive for the opening of Goebbels' speech at 4 p.m., and, much to their surprise, met little opposition. Darling, who was last man to arrive at Berlin, was seen to be getting rather more flak and was shot down over or near the city. One pilot, already in a homeward power descent, saw a fighter a long way behind which eventually disappeared without attacking.'

'*No.* 109 *Squadron, Wyton*

Wyton is the headquarters of the Pathfinder Force, commanded by Group Capt. Bennett, and 109 Squadron's Mosquitoes are beginning to play an important part in the Force's doings. The C.O., Wing Commander MacMullin, and his henchman, Sqd. Ldr. Bufton, are old hands at special radio: the present Mosquito installations are, to a large extent, due to their efforts. Broadly speaking, these installations enable aircraft crews to fix their position any-where within a radius of about 250 miles with extreme accuracy without looking outside the cockpit—accuracy not in terms of miles, but of yards (the enthusiasts say feet). This degree of accuracy has been proved by very many tests over chosen objectives in this country, but at the present stage of development there is no doubt that, under operating conditions, cumulative errors will at times be large. We have proofs now of inaccurate, but also of extremely accurate bombing by this means.'

This 'Pathfinder' technique made an enormous difference to the heavy bomber force in enabling really accurate bombing to be carried out. It is pure common sense to realize that young, relatively inexperienced pilots in heavy bombers failed repeatedly to find their target on a dark misty night, constantly harassed by enemy flak and enemy fighters. They did their best in an almost impossible task. But there is little doubt that many thousands of bombs were dropped as much as thirty miles from the target. The Pathfinder force altered all this and took an enormous strain off the bomber crews who had the added satisfaction of knowing their bombs had been delivered on the target.

Feb./March 1943

'Since starting range patrols, this Squadron has shot up over 30 trains, damaged six electrical transformers and severely damaged a 1,500-ton ship. S/Ldr. Maxwell recently flew all the way home from the north coast of Spain on one engine, a distance of nearly 500 miles, at 180 m.p.h.'

'From January 1st 1943 to March 31st, Mosquitoes' "bag" of enemy aircraft consists of the following:

> Destroyed 7
> Probably ,, 3
> Damaged 2

The fuel cost works out at about 187,000 gallons of petrol per German aircraft destroyed.'

'*No.* 109 *Squadron, Wyton.* The peculiar looking scientists of T.R.E., the personnel of 109 Squadron, the de Havilland Aircraft Co., Ltd., and Air Commodore Bennett, D.S.O., can collectively claim a major victory in this war in enabling the Lancasters, Stirlings and Halifaxes of Bomber Command to drop bombs accurately on both visible and invisible targets.

Up to the time that 109's Pathfinder Mosquitoes got going in January 1943, only three bombs out of a few thousand aimed at it, had actually hit Krupps' works at Essen. Since then the place has been accurately plastered with incendiaries and four-thousand-pounders, and the cost involved in its final destruction can now be fairly accurately assessed.

In addition to Krupps, Mosquito Pathfinders have positioned enormous bomb loads at St. Nazaire and Lorient.

We have recently completed our part of the work on one of these aircraft necessitated by a modification which it is hoped will still further increase the accuracy and scope of these operations.'

April/May 1943

'Mosquitoes have flown all the way home from Norway, Berlin, Bordeaux, Karlsruhe, Jena and Essen on one engine.'

Quotation from an R.A.F. Officer:

'In conclusion, the Mosquito represents all that is finest in aeronautical design. It is an aeroplane that could only have been conceived in this country, and combines the British genius for building a practical and straightforward machine with the typical de Havilland flair for producing a first-rate aeroplane that looks right and *is* right.'

Appendix I

June 1943

'Besides attacks on enemy aircraft, Mosquitoes, during June, sank a trawler and shot up five surfaced submarines in the Bay of Biscay, in two cases killing some of the crews; the submarines put up intense defensive fire.'

August/Sept. 1943

'4,000-*lb. Bomb Installation.* Orders have been received to incorporate this in bomber types both retrospectively and on the production line. Either the G.P., M.C., or H.C. type 4,000-lb. bomb can be carried at will, and the change over to or from the standard load of 4×500-lb. bombs can be made in under one hour.

Mark XVI aircraft so fitted will start coming off the production line in November next; this is a remarkable achievement by the Production and Design Departments.'

Nov./Dec. 1943

'Engine failures during the month, due to failure of petrol to reach the carburettor, became so serious that all Mk. IX aircraft were banned from operational flying until certain modifications, including the blanking of the fuel cooler, had been incorporated.'

January 1944

'*Nitrous Oxide Injection.* On the night of January 2/3 John Cunningham flew his Mk. XIII Mosquito with N_2O injection on operations for the first time and bagged a M.E.410. He had the gas on for two minutes (which gave on test, a computed increase of 41 m.p.h. at 27,000 feet) and he caught the Hun near the French coast.'

'Up to the end of January 1944, No. 23 had destroyed 33 enemy aircraft in flight, 39 on the ground and 331 locomotives.'

Appendix I

'*Fatal Accidents.* There were ten fatal accidents during January, mainly due to piloting errors. Four cases of reputed structural failure in flight are under investigation by the A.I.B.'

February/March 1944

'John Cunningham has now left 85 Squadron and gone to No. 11 Group at Uxbridge as Night Operations Controller. His squadron has been taken over by Wing Commander Miller, D.F.C.'

A pilot's combat report states:

'Approaching St. Yan from the North, I climbed to 500 ft., instantly seeing three a/c on the A/F. As we crossed the north perimeter we passed over about 50 men in dark uniform, all walking in the same direction looking up at us. My Obs., glancing at F/L Cleveland going in for his attack saw black smoke pouring from his engines, and believed that he had been hit. He was opening his mouth to yell at me to turn and get revenge by shooting up these Huns, when the smoke ceased and he realized that it had been caused by the extra boost necessary for the attack. I opened fire at range of 600 yards on the two E/A on the left side, both cannon and M/G, seeing strikes immediately on one of them. As I closed, the other one burst into flames. F/L Cleveland, who was behind, saw a petrol bowser go up in flames, and the first E/A attacked also burst into flames. As we closed we had identified them as JU.52s. The E.A. on the right of the others was an 86, and I left this to F/Lt. Cleveland, and my observer saw this E/A go up in flames, as I was pulling up through the flames of the two JU.52s. After setting course, I looked to see how much film had been used and found camera not switched on. We headed south for twenty miles, then set course for Dole/Tavaux having difficulty in finding the A/F as rivers appeared swollen (probably in flood) in

228

comparison with their size. My observer, by excellent navigation, brought us to the town of Dole and we there encountered the Bi-Heinkel with its satellites. Owing to the low speed of the targets, I found it impossible in my climb to get into position to attack. I broke off and was delighted to see F/Lt. Cleveland knocking off the rear glider. I manœuvred and came up behind the remaining glider and Heinkel I, taking cine-camera shots as I closed. When the glider filled the ring-sight I gave it a short burst (2 secs.). Pieces blew off, and I was very concerned in dodging the debris, I saw him going down out of control. I closed behind the Heinkel, opened fire and immediately saw strikes on two engines (3 to 4 secs.). I broke off and F/Lt. Cleveland carried on the attack. When he had finished, I came in and gave him a burst of M/G as he was slipping to earth. As I passed over him his starboard engines and fuselage were burning fiercely on the ground. It had crashed port wing down.

As the Bi-Heinkel consists of two 'separate' Heinkels, it is requested that a claim of one H.E. 111 destroyed each, be allowed to F/Lt. Scherf and F/Lt. Cleveland.'

'*No. 8 Group, Bomber Command.* Several squadrons in this Group operating Mk. IVs and IXs have been carrying 4,000-lb. bombs to Germany with great success; the great cry at the moment is for more aircraft. No complaints have been received of poor fore and aft stability, although 692 squadron at Graveley found on one Mk. IV that they could not get it above 20,000 ft. on full load, so it has been relegated to a training flight. Most of the bombing when carrying 4,000-lb. bombs is done at between 23,000 and 25,000 ft.

Two Canadian Mk. XXs have been operating with 139 at Upwood, and both have now done over 100 hours with very little trouble—the pilots who fly them reckon they are faster than English Mk. IVs.'

'The Reconnaissance Wing of the 8th U.S.A.A.C. under

Colonel Roosevelt based at Cheddington near Tring are now starting to receive their first Mk. XVIs. All personnel are very thrilled at getting Mosquitoes, and in time they hope to get between 50 and 60 aircraft. Before being delivered to Cheddington, the Mosquitoes go to an American M.U. at Burtonwood in Lancashire for installation of special equipment—the main duties of this wing will be photographic reconnaissance, and meteorological reports. Several of the American pilots and ground crews have already been over to Hatfield, and around our dispersal factories. Previous to having Mosquitoes this wing have operated Liberators and Lightnings.'

March/April 1944

'*Air Expeditionary Attack Force.* South of England aerodromes are crowded with single-seater fighter squadrons of every type, living under canvas, and now well practised in mobility. Several Mosquito squadrons are also under canvas and prepared for a quick move, but they will obviously take advantage of home bases as long as possible. When the time comes, the first to operate from Continental bases will be Fighter Bombers and Night Fighters of No. 2 and No. 85 Groups respectively. Group Captain Wyckham-Barnes is in command of one of the Fighter Bomber Wings, and a better man for the job would be hard to find. These Fighter Bomber units will operate at night to a large extent, shadowing and strafing enemy mobile divisions.'

'Mosquitoes were recently detailed to bomb a prison camp in France containing 40 French hostages who were to be shot next morning, the idea being that some of those not blown up might escape. According to subsequent intelligence reports 10 were killed or badly hurt and all the rest did get away with the help of agents.'

Appendix I

'*Deck Landing Trials*. On May 9/10 Mosquito trials were completed on H.M.S. *Indefatigable* near Ailsa Craig. Starting at 18,000 lb. the all-up weight was progressively increased to 22,000 lb. for take-off and 20,000 for landing on; the reduction for landing was made by dropping four live 500-lb. bombs into the sea unpleasantly close to a small fishing boat the pilot hadn't seen.

All take-offs and landings were successful: on one full load landing the arrester hook locked "up" after hitting the deck without picking up a wire; the pilot, Cmdr. Lans, jammed his brakes on and pulled up with 160 feet of deck to spare, which inspired a lot of confidence after the excitement died down.

One's general impression of these trials was that considerable skill is required to land a Mosquito on a carrier under average conditions.'

'In one month, July 15th–August 15th, Mosquitoes dropped 336 four-thousand-pound bombs on Berlin; during the same period 818 flying bombs landed in Greater London out of 2,493 launched.'

(When flying bombs started to come over from the enemy, Mosquitoes found a new job because they were fast enough to catch and shoot down these vermin in large numbers. Our single-seater fighters also accounted for big quantities.)

*

In reading through my brother's complete volume of notes covering more than three years of Mosquito operation, the two main facts left on my mind were, firstly the relatively great success achieved by the Royal Air Force in operating the 'plane, and secondly, the appalling list of casualties even with a 'plane that was considered 'outstanding' not only by those flying it, but also by the enemy.

Appendix I

In 1956 Herr Ernst Heinkel, the German designer, sent me a copy of his book *He.1000* in which he states:

'The British, with the de Havilland Mosquito, night after night, undeterred by slower fighters, bombed Berlin and other German cities.'

Later in the book he writes:

'The aim was to get into mass production a machine that would meet the demands made by night flying against the enemy bomber squadrons, and particularly one that would cope with the fabulously fast R.A.F. Mosquito.'

But due to jealousy, bickerings, the lack of real hope for victory and the general breakdown of German industry, the 'plane never reached the production stage.

The numerous hazards of all kinds which are inescapable in any war will usually produce an appalling casualty list and a wastage of material on a colossal scale. In the case of the Mosquito these losses were reduced due to its generally superior performance especially in speed, but they were still considerable. Enemy losses were, of course, on a much vaster scale.

I doubt whether the design and building of the Mosquito taught us much that could be usefully applied to the design of civil aircraft. The problems of the warplane and the airliner are totally different. When we started the design of the all-metal Comet airliner we had to adopt an entirely new line of thought as regards design and also in construction.

INDEX

Index

Index

Index

MacMillan, Wing Commander Norman, 91

MacMullin, Wing Commander, 224

MacRobertson England-Australia International Air Race, 151–3

Marconi Instruments Ltd., 206

Markham, Beryl, 141

Maxim, Hiram, 47

Medley Manor, Oxford, 15–18, 24, 25, 26, 28, 36, 45, 48, 199, 200–1

Mercedes car, 35

Messerschmitt aircraft, 168, 227

Military Aircraft Trials, 77, 91

Mollison, Mr. and Mrs. Jim, 140, 151, 152

Moore-Brabazon, J. T. C. *See* Lord Brabazon of Tara

Mordaunt, Ann (Mrs. Darrell), 198

Mordaunt, Joan. *See* Lady Joan de Havilland

Mordaunt, Philip, 198

Morris, W. R. *See* Lord Nuffield

Mors cars, 40

Motor Omnibus Construction Co., 52

Napier Lion engine, 113

Night Fighter, 174

Nixon, Wilfred E., 101–2, 111, 112, 144, 194

Norman, Jim, 119

Norman, Sir Nigel, 125

Norway, Nevil Shute, 143

Nuffield, Lord (W. R. Morris), 48

Nulli Secundus airship, 78, 79

O'Gorman, Mervyn ('O.G.'), 67–69, 72–73, 87, 90, 91, 92

Oxford Electric Light Co., 36

Panhard cars, 32–34, 39, 40, 56, 62

Pardoe, Geoffrey, 204

Parke, Wilfred, 91

Parker, 'Clench', 23, 24

Paulhan, Louis, 55, 93

Pégoud, Adolphe, 87

Pioneer of the Air, 80n

Plumb, Fred, 163

Pullinger, T. C. *See* B.H.P.

Raphael, Wing Commander, 223

Rawnsley and Wright, 174n

R.E.1 aircraft, 83

R.E.P. engine, 70

Renault cars, 40

Renault engines, 77, 119, 121

Richards, Tony, 175

Roe, Sir Alliot Verdon, 47, 54, 65

Rolls, The Hon. C. S., 39

Rolls-Royce Ltd., 163, 189, 206, 207

Rolls-Royce Eagle engine, 98, 99

Rolls-Royce Falcon engine, 114

Rolls-Royce Merlin engine, 156, 159, 160, 162, 163, 165

Rolls-Royce R.B.163 engine, 196

Rossmore, Lord, 137

Royal Aero Club, 73, 74, 136

Royal Air Force, 101, 104, 107, 111, 116, 117, 125, 160, 164, 165, 166, 173, 174, 186, 191

Royal Air Force Bomber Command, 222, 226

R.A.F. Mosquito Squadrons.
No. 1 P.R.U. Benson, 218, 219; Leuchars, 221, 222
No. 85 N.F. Hunsdon, 223
No. 109 Pathfinder, Wyton, 223, 224, 225, 226

Index

Nos. 105 and 139 Bomber, Marham, 221, 223, 224
No. 157 N.F. Castle Camps, 223
Royal Aircraft Establishment. *See* Farnborough
Royal Aircraft Factory. *See* Farnborough
Royal Automobile Club, 105
Royal Canadian Air Force, 186
Royal Flying Corps (R.F.C.), 77, 95, 97, 103, 105, 107, 135, 166
Royce, Henry, 39
Rubin, Bernard, 151
Rugby (Oakfield School), 24, 29, 35, 36

S.51 Satellite, 207
St. Barbe, Francis E. N., 102–3, 111, 112, 114, 144, 194
Salisbury Hall, 158–9, 163
Santos-Dumont, A., 47
Santos-Dumont aircraft. *See* S.E.1
Saunders, Anna (maternal grandmother), 15, 17, 48, 49
Saunders, Jason (maternal grandfather), 15–17, 22, 24, 26, 30, 32, 36, 48–49, 50, 69, 201
Scott, Charles, 151, 152, 153
Scott, Peter, 199
S.E. aircraft (Scout Experimental), 74
S.E.1 aircraft (Santos-Dumont Experimental), 74, 75
Seely, General, 82
Serpollet steam cars, 34
Seven Barrows, 14, 27, 54, 56, 59–60, 66, 69, 74
Short Stirling aircraft, 226
Shute, Nevil. *See* Norway, Nevil Shute
Siddeley, John, 42

Siddeley Puma engine, 119
Slade, Wing Commander Gordon, 219
Slessor, Marshal of the R.A.F., Sir John, 220
Smith, J. Philip, 148
Smith-Barry, Major R. R., 65
Sopwith, Sir Thomas, O.M., 192
Sperry Gyroscope Co., 206
Spicer, Dorothy, 139
Spooner, Winifred, 141
Spratt, Norman, 78, 87
Stanley steam cars, 34
Stockley, Colonel Charles F., 198
Stowe School, 127
Supermarine Spitfire aircraft, 149, 163
Sykes, Sir Frederick, 77, 105
Sykes, Lady, 77

Tewin, 711–2
Thomas, George Holt, 93–95, 97, 99, 101, 104, 108, 112, 113, 114
Thomas, Lottie, 127
Thomas, Louie. *See* Lady Louie de Havilland
Thomas, Sir Miles, 181
Thomson, Sir George, 78
Thor missile, 207
Tiltman, A. Hessell, 143
Tizard, Sir Henry, 107
Trenchard, Viscount, 77, 105–7, 117

U.A.T. (Union Aeromaritime de Transport), 186
Udet, E., 131, 132

Vickers Ltd., 103
Vickers R.100 airship, 143
Vickers Scout aircraft, 103

Index